P9-DTM-412

DATE DUE

			PRINTED IN U.S.A.

ACKNOWLEDGMENTS

Thanks are due to a number of people who have made substantial contributions to this new, and completely revised, ninth edition of *Resumes That Get Jobs*. Linda Bernbach, Executive Editor of Arco Publishing, provided opportunity, encouragement, and advice. Janet Stumper turned my words into a book with her graphic design skills. Art Ungar, of Success Strategies in Lawrenceville, New Jersey, and Marilyn Silverman, of Word Center Printing in Hamilton Square, New Jersey, shared their expertise in resume preparation. John Nebesney drew the witty illustrations with good humor of his own.

Most of all, my thanks go to Saundra Young and Travis Potter for their understanding, patience, and love.

Ray Potter
Hopewell, New Jersey

RESUMES THAT GET JOBS

Jean Reed

Revised and expanded by Ray Potter

Riverside Community College
Library
4800 Magnolia Avenue
Riverside, California 92506

REF HF 5383 .R4 1998

Reed, Jean.

Resumes that get jobs

Dedicated to Saundra and Travis with love and gratitude

Ninth Edition

Copyright © 1998, 1995 by ARCO Publishing,
a division of Simon & Schuster, Inc.
All rights reserved
including the right of reproduction
in whole or in part in any form.

Macmillan Reference USA
A Simon & Schuster Macmillan Company
1633 Broadway
New York, NY 10019-6785

An Arco Book

MACMILLAN is a registered trademark of Macmillan, Inc.
ARCO is a registered trademark of Simon & Schuster, Inc.

ISBN 0-02-862206-5

Manufactured in the United States of America.

10   9   8   7   6   5   4   3   2   1

PREFACE

WHAT THIS BOOK CAN DO FOR YOU

All resumes are not equal. Some are simply better than others. It doesn't have anything to do with the backgrounds that are described on them or the talents of the people who wrote them. It's just that some resumes get attention. They communicate with potential employers. They speak directly to the needs of the people doing the hiring. This book can teach you how to write that kind of resume—resumes that get jobs. Step by step, you will learn how to write the best resume for the job you want. It's surprisingly easy. It's not painful or mysterious or filled with drudgery. You might even enjoy it!

Not all resume-writing books are equal either. Most of them are terribly out of date. The resumes they produce seem old fashioned in today's job market. They make the people who write them seem old fashioned too. Many resume-writing books seem almost interchangeable. They offer the same old advice that they did twenty years ago. That advice isn't going to land you a job today.

Job seekers today need every advantage they can get. Finding a job is an incredibly competitive process. Your resume can help you stand out from the competition—not by being overly flashy or garish, but by meeting the needs of the person who is looking for help. It can help you get a foot in the door, one step ahead of your competitors. This is the kind of resume that you can write with a little help from this book. You will be pleased with the resume you create—and so will your future employer.

Everything you need to prepare your resume is included in the book. There are clear instructions, worksheets for each step along the way, and even lists of words you can use that have real impact with prospective employers. Just as importantly, the whole approach described here reflects the latest marketing techniques. The best person to "market" you is you. You have a thorough and intimate knowledge of your "product." You know its capabilities and its potential. You know where and how it performs best. And your "product" is unique. No one else has exactly your qualifications, your experience, your skills, your background. Whether you are entering the job market for the first time, changing jobs, switching career fields, or reentering the job market after an absence, with the guidance you find in this book you can become a successful marketer—of yourself. You can sell yourself into a job.

This new edition contains a significant new chapter that will help you stay one step ahead of your competitors in the job market. Entitled "Electronic Resumes," it is a thorough guide to how to prepare a resume that can be successfully "read" by computers. This is essential today because employers, large and small, have discovered that computers are much better at storing and retrieving resumes than humans are. Only a few short years ago, the resumes of job seekers were stored in file cabinets (or in boxes or sometimes on the shelves of storerooms). When a job became available it meant that someone had to go through the files (or boxes or shelves) to find resumes of candidates who looked like they could handle the job. It was a very haphazard process and, of course, the results weren't very good.

For many employers, the process of finding qualified candidates for jobs has changed immensely. Now they let their computers do the work of filing and finding resumes. With their applicant tracking systems, they "scan" resumes into computerized storage. Now when they have job openings, they simply enter a description of the ideal candidates and their computers produce lists of applicants who meet the qualifications. Resumes can be called up and viewed directly on screen and can be quickly transmitted to other computers throughout a company.

Although this may sound rather impersonal, it is actually a terrific asset for job seekers. It means that you might be considered for many more jobs than you know! If you understand how to create a resume that is likely to be discovered in those computerized searches, you will greatly expand your chances of being included on the lists of qualified candidates—even for jobs that you didn't know were available. The newly-added chapter on "Electronic Resumes" will show you how to construct a resume that will get noticed—by computers as well as by humans!

Resumes That Get Jobs is a very useful book. It will help you create your own best resume, all by yourself. It will guide you through every step. And the process is simple, straightforward, and painless. What are you waiting for? Let's get started!

TABLE OF CONTENTS

INTRODUCTION..9

CHAPTER 1 KNOW YOURSELF: YOUR PERSONAL SKILLS...................11

CHAPTER 2 KNOWING EVEN MORE: YOUR PERSONAL
QUALIFICATIONS..19

CHAPTER 3 "WORK EXPERIENCE": DESCRIBING YOUR "WORK"........23

CHAPTER 4 ACCOMPLISHMENTS: DESCRIBING YOUR
"ACHIEVEMENTS"..33

CHAPTER 5 JOB SKILLS: DESCRIBING "ON THE JOB" SKILLS.............37

CHAPTER 6 QUALIFICATIONS SUMMARY: A CAPSULE
DESCRIPTION OF YOURSELF..............................41

CHAPTER 7 EDUCATION: SUMMARIZING YOUR EDUCATION
AND TRAINING..43

CHAPTER 8 AWARDS: RECORDING RECOGNITION...................... 51

CHAPTER 9 MEMBERSHIPS: ASSOCIATIONS, CLUBS, AND
ORGANIZATIONS..53

CHAPTER 10 PUBLICATIONS: YOUR WRITTEN WORDS........................55

CHAPTER 11 PERSONAL INFORMATION: USING INFORMATION
TO YOUR ADVANTAGE......................................57

CHAPTER 12 REFERENCES: WHAT THEY ARE AND HOW TO
USE THEM..59

CHAPTER 13   YOUR JOB OBJECTIVE: WHAT DO YOU WANT
(AND WHAT CAN YOU CONTRIUTE)?............................ 63

CHAPTER 14   ELECTRONIC RESUMES: YOUR RESUME IN THE
AGE OF COMPUTERS... 67

CHAPTER 15   ASSEMBLING YOUR RESUME: PUTTING IT ALL
TOGETHER!... 83

CHAPTER 16   PRINTING YOUR RESUME: HOW TO GET
THE BEST RESULTS... 89

CHAPTER 17   COVER LETTERS: BUILDING BRIDGES BETWEEN
RESUMES AND JOBS... 95

CHAPTER 18   RESUME TIPS: WHAT TO DO AND WHAT
NOT TO DO...105

CHAPTER 19   SAMPLE RESUMES...107

CHAPTER 20   SAMPLE RESUME INDEX 206

INTRODUCTION

WHAT IS A RESUME?

A resume is a selected summary of significant facts about you. Take a minute to look at the key words in that statement. A resume doesn't present everything there is to know about you. It presents selected significant facts and it serves them up in a neatly packaged summary. To write a resume, then, you need to know which facts about you are significant to a prospective employer. You need to know how to summarize them so that your next employer can see quickly why you are the right person for the job. And you need to know how to present them on paper.

Sounds pretty simple, right? Well, it is. There are only two things you have to know to write a great resume: yourself and your future employer. If you know yourself (and who doesn't?), you're halfway there. If you know your prospective employer (and you will soon, if you don't already), you can write a resume that will get noticed.

WHAT DO RESUMES DO?

Strictly speaking, resumes don't get jobs. Resumes get interviews. And interviews get jobs. You won't get an interview without a resume. And you won't get a job offer without an interview. But the resume is the first step to a job.

Resumes save employers the time and trouble of meeting everyone who is interested in working for them. Instead of meeting face to face, they "meet" on paper. Since you don't get to talk at this first "meeting" (you're not even there!), your resume has to answer the kinds of questions that employers ask as they look over resumes. Can this person do the job? Can this person make a contribution beyond just "doing the job"? Is this person qualified? What kind of person is this applicant? (There are many more questions, but you get the idea.)

Resumes can't answer every question that employers have. If they could, there would be no need for interviews. However, the resumes that can answer the most questions, and answer them positively, are those that are going to make it to the pile marked "INTERVIEW." You have probably heard that employers who are looking through resumes sort them into three piles: NO (also known as "The Rejects Pile"); MAYBE (to be looked over again if there aren't enough resumes in the next pile); and YES (the resumes that are marked "INTERVIEW"). What you've heard is true; that's exactly how it usually works. Your goal, obviously, is to get your resume into the "YES" pile and be invited in for an interview.

A successful resume is one that leads to interviews. Interviews lead directly to jobs. Writing your resume is the first—and most important—step you can take toward getting a job. It is worth doing well because the reward is so big. Do a great job on your resume and it can lead you to a great job!

ANYONE CAN WRITE A RESUME

You don't have to be a terrific writer to write a terrific resume. Terrific writers write books. Anyone can write a resume. And it seems like everyone needs a resume today. In the sample resumes at the back of this book you will find resumes from electricians, police officers, secretaries, teachers, lawyers, counselors, and business executives—and many, many more. Most of these people wrote their resumes themselves (some of them had a little help from the author). None of them was a wonderful writer. None of them had some sort of special talent for writing resumes. They were people, just like you, who needed resumes. They wrote theirs—and you can write yours. All you need is this book and a pencil. It really is that easy.

So grab a pencil and you're on your way.

1 KNOW YOURSELF
YOUR PERSONAL SKILLS

We promised that *Resumes That Get Jobs* would take you step by step through the process of creating your own best resume. We also stated that there were only two things that you needed to know to write your best resume. The first one is: know yourself. That's where we're going to start. Here you will begin to answer the question that is always in the front of every employer's mind: "What can this person do for me?"

Like many of the sections that follow, this first chapter includes easy-to-use worksheets. After you read the brief text in each section, fill out the worksheets. These worksheets are the "building blocks" of your resume. When you have completed the worksheets you will be ready to start "constructing" your resume. This building-block approach will make it possible for you to assemble resumes for yourself—not just one resume, but a different resume every time you need a new one. It's a very flexible system, and it's very simple too. (If you have borrowed this book from a library or from a friend, you should photocopy the worksheets and write on the copies. Better yet, buy a copy of the book for yourself and then you can write in it as much as you want to!)

THE IMPORTANCE OF KNOWING YOURSELF

The most important information you need to build your resume is knowledge about what you have to offer to an employer. In the past, resumes reported only on-the-job experience. This approach helped those people who had been employed already and who were planning to take another step on the same career path. Everybody else—those who were looking for a first job, those who were reentering the workforce, those who were trying to change careers, those trying to leap up the corporate ladder without climbing it rung by rung, and many others—was hurt by this working-experience approach to resumes. From the viewpoint of employers, the jobs-only emphasis wasn't all that useful either.

What employers learned from traditional resumes was only what an applicant had done in the past and not what that applicant could do in the future.

Employers have always known that some of their best employees have been people whose past experiences didn't lead them very directly to their current positions. But they have also been afraid to take chances in hiring new employees who haven't already performed exactly the same job somewhere else. Even the most open-minded employer hasn't known how to spot potentially great employees who might have the skills to do a job but lack the direct experience.

Resume writing styles haven't helped. Most resumes today look a lot like resumes from thirty years ago. The world of work has changed a lot in the last thirty years, but you wouldn't know it to look at most resumes. And employers are still left trying to guess what the people behind these resumes have to offer.

This is one of the many places where this book is different. It begins by helping you to analyze your skills. As you will discover, skills are one of the "bridges" that allow you to cross from one type of job—even one type of career—to another.

GETTING TO KNOW YOUR SKILLS

You may not know it right now, but you have a unique set of skills. You have acquired them in every activity in which you have ever participated. Not all skills come from your past jobs (although you may have plenty of job skills as well). You have collected skills in volunteer work, in working at home, in being a student, in your hobbies, and in your extracurricular activities.

Skills are often transferable from one occupation to another. For example, teachers frequently say to career counselors: "I'm a teacher. What skills do I have besides teaching?" The answer is: "You have a lot!" And they do. Teachers have skills like time planning, motivating, supervising, setting goals, evaluating results, public speaking, and many others. So do you.

The skills worksheets that follow are designed to help you identify your particular skills. They begin by asking you to list a specific activity which has been significant to you. You can start with your most recent job or you can start with any other role that has been important for you. If you really can't think of a place to start, simply list the activity that takes up most of your time each day (besides sleeping!).

You will be asked to describe the activity. Write this description in the way you might say it to an employer if you were asked in an interview, "Tell me a little bit about that." It doesn't have to be polished or precise right now, because you will have an opportunity to rewrite it later.

NAMING YOUR SKILLS

Next you will identify the skills you used or learned in the activity you selected. Some of the skills you list are skills that you already had when you began the activity. You may have learned these in school, from a previous job, from your parents, or just from living. All of these "count" here. All are important. If you find yourself listing skills that you don't want to use on a job, drop these and concentrate on those that you would be comfortable discussing with an employer. For example, if one of your activities has been to raise a child from infancy to kindergarten, you might have acquired undeniable skills in changing diapers. However, if you are not looking for a job in child care, this is a skill that won't be much in demand. Focus instead on the time planning, household management, and related skills that you had to employ in child rearing.

Following the worksheets is a sample list of skills you can refer to after you make your own list, in case you forgot to include some of the skills you used or learned. There are three skills worksheets included. You can complete fewer than three or do more if you want (photocopy the worksheets or use your own sheets of paper if you want to analyze more than three activities).

THE SKILLS SUMMARY

After you have identified skills for your activities, you will be ready to fill out the "Skills Summary" worksheet. Here you will be asked to look over the skills that you recorded for each activity and to take a look at the sample list too. From these, you will select the personal skills that you would like a prospective employer to know you have. Don't worry now about how you will use these in your resume. That will become clear later. For now, fill out the worksheets and the summary and congratulate yourself on accomplishing a feat that few resume writers have been able to accomplish!

SKILLS WORKSHEET

Activity (This can be a job, a volunteer activity, a hobby, a project, etc.)

_____

_____

_____

_____

Description of the activity (Briefly describe what you did.)

_____

_____

_____

_____

Skills you used or learned in the activity _____

_____

_____

_____

_____

_____

_____

(Refer to the sample list of skills after you have made your own and add any from the list that you haven't included already.)

SKILLS WORKSHEET

Activity (This can be a job, a volunteer activity, a hobby, a project, etc.)

_____

_____

_____

_____

Description of the activity (Briefly describe what you did.)

_____

_____

_____

_____

Skills you used or learned in the activity _____

_____

_____

_____

_____

(Refer to the sample list of skills after you have made your own and add any from the list that you haven't included already.)

SKILLS WORKSHEET

Activity (This can be a job, a volunteer activity, a hobby, a project, etc.)

_____

_____

_____

_____

Description of the activity (Briefly describe what you did.)

_____

_____

_____

_____

Skills you used or learned in the activity _____

_____

_____

_____

_____

(Refer to the sample list of skills after you have made your own and add any from the list that you haven't included already.)

SAMPLE LIST OF SKILLS

You use skills and learn skills in every activity, whether it is a job, a hobby, a volunteer position, or working around the house or apartment. Usually you can identify your skills just by concentrating on the activity and thinking about the skills that it required. This sample list is included here to stimulate your thinking. It doesn't pretend to be comprehensive, but it should trigger your thoughts as you analyze your activities. Refer to this list as you complete the Skills Worksheets and the Skills Summary.

Planning	Supervising
Leading	Coordinating
Communicating	Analyzing
Persuading	Selling
Coaching	Counseling
Teaching	Instructing
Solving problems	Finding solutions
Resolving conflicts	Keeping records
Motivating	Mediating
Writing	Explaining
Creating	Innovating
Attending to details	Decision making
Budgeting	Bookkeeping
Managing time	Tracking details
Increasing productivity	Increasing profit
Stimulating growth	Stimulating sales

SKILLS SUMMARY

From the skills you identified on the skills worksheets and from the sample list of skills, note below those skills that you would like a prospective employer to know you have. For each skill that you include, ask yourself one question: Will I be comfortable talking with a future employer about this? If the answer is no, drop it from your list of skills. If you're not sure about the answer to the question, leave it on your list for now.

1. _____

2. _____

3. _____

4. _____

5. _____

6. _____

7. _____

8. _____

9. _____

10. _____

2 KNOWING EVEN MORE
YOUR PERSONAL QUALIFICATIONS

Congratulations! You have completed the first step in creating your own best resume! Now it's time to move on to the next chapter and explore your "Personal Qualifications."

Just as you have a unique collection of skills, you have your own set of personal qualifications. People often refer to their qualifications as "aspects of my personality." You might say: "That's just who I am." Well, who are you? That's what you need to put down on paper under the heading of personal qualifications. Look at this as if you were someone else—maybe your best friend—describing you. What would you say?

Personal qualifications are sometimes called "traits" or "qualities." They are usually best described with short phrases, like: quick learner; good with my hands; can talk to just about anybody; pleasant personality; always keep cool under pressure; able to do many things at once, etc. Don't think of these only as job related. You are trying to describe yourself to someone who has never met you. You're creating a "word picture" of yourself.

Of course, you're trying to emphasize the positive here. You can leave out the negative aspects of your personality. This is not the place to note, for example, "I'm a real hothead" or "I drive people nuts with my constant talking." These may be aspects of your personality, but they're not what we're looking for here!

If you find it difficult to describe your personal qualifications, even after you have tried to look at yourself as your best friend might look at you, it's time to ask your best friend for help. Ask that friend (better yet, ask two or three) to describe your best qualities. Take notes while your friend is talking and then transfer your notes to the worksheet. (After all, what are friends for if not to tell you what they think is best about you?) There is a list of sample personal qualifications right after the worksheet, in case you want to add to your list. But don't go right to this sample list. You (and your best friend) can describe you much better than the list can.

PERSONAL QUALIFICATIONS WORKSHEET

What are your best personal qualities? (Briefly describe them with a word or a phrase.)

1. _____

2. _____

3. _____

4. _____

5. _____

6. _____

7. _____

8. _____

9. _____

10. _____

(Refer to the sample list after you have made your own and add any from that list that you haven't included already.)

Congratulations! You have completed the second step in creating your own best resume! Now it's time to move on to the next section.

PERSONAL QUALIFICATIONS

The descriptive words below are only a sample of the kinds of words you might use to describe yourself. They can be used to trigger your own thoughts about your best qualities. Refer to this list when you are filling out your Personal Qualifications Worksheet.

Reliable	Dependable
Well-organized	Quick learner
Self-motivated	Self-starter
Imaginative	Bright
Smart	Intelligent
Thorough	Conscientious
Persuasive	Diplomatic
Friendly	Outgoing
Loyal	Persistent
Practical	Problem-solver
Active	Calm
Trustworthy	Inquisitive
Dedicated	Giving
Methodical	Productive
Creative	Ingenious
Clever	Original
Systematic	Businesslike
Professional	Honest

Unique	Skilled
Talented	Adept
Able	Competent
Efficient	Proficient
Exceptional	Congenial
Devoted	Energetic
Aggressive	Assertive
Genial	Gregarious
Truthful	Composed
Patient	Tenacious
Poised	Even-tempered
Astute	Incisive
Perceptive	Rational
Curious	Discerning
Sensible	Thoughtful
Precise	Flexible
Insightful	Caring
Versatile	Responsible
Analytic	Organized

3 "WORK EXPERIENCE"

DESCRIBING YOUR "WORK"

Once you have completed the Personal Skills Worksheets, the Skills Summary, and the Personal Qualifications Worksheet, you have put part of yourself down on paper. Let's call that the "personal part" of you. Now it's time to turn your attention to what we might call the "public part" of you. This is where you get to describe your experience in specific jobs—or in other positions of responsibility. Actually, you have already started this process by identifying "activities" when you filled out your Personal Skills Worksheets. You will start in a similar way here.

"WORK EXPERIENCE"

"Work experience" is in quotation marks because the name isn't exactly right. What we're actually talking about here is just "experience," but not every experience you have had in your life. In this section, you will focus on your experiences that are "work-like," whether or not you actually got paid or had a formal job. These may be the experiences that gave you some of the "personal skills" you have already recorded—the experiences that we called "activities" in the section where you analyzed your skills.

Completing the "Work Experience" Worksheets is a three-stage process. First you will describe the experience; then you will add "action words"; and, finally, you will put in "facts and figures." With each "Work Experience" Worksheet you complete, you will have added another "building block" for constructing your resume.

If you have held jobs, you will probably want to use those jobs—and job titles—on your "Work Experience" worksheets. If you have not worked (or haven't worked in the last ten years or more), you will want to use the kind of experience you used on your Skills Worksheet: a volunteer or unpaid position, a part-time job, a summer job, an internship or "co-op" position, a job in the home, etc. In fact, if you have held a responsible position as a volunteer, you may want to add this to your list of experiences even if you have been employed at a full-time job as well. Employers like to know what people do outside their jobs; if you have been able to hold a significant volunteer position, it says something positive about you.

The "Work Experience" Worksheets are easy to use. First, fill in the top of the form. Start with your present job or position on the first worksheet and then work backwards chronologically through your previous jobs or activities. List the main responsibilities of your position next to the numbers. Begin with your most important responsibility next to number one and work down in priority if you can. (If you can't put your responsibilities into a ranked order very easily, don't worry about it. Any order is fine for now.)

ADDING "ACTION WORDS"

Once you have recorded the key tasks of your position, use the next section of the form to re-word these tasks so that they include action words. These are essential to the success of your resume. Ideally, the descriptions of your positions will consist of short phrases that each begin with an action word. There is a list of sample action words at the end of the "Work Experience" Worksheets. You can take words from this list or use your own words. The secrets here are to keep the phrases brief and the first words "strong."

For example, you might have said in the first section of the worksheet: "As the assistant to the purchasing manager, I make sure that bid forms go out to possible vendors and then I record the bids when they come back in. I have an assistant who takes care of the filing and the mailing." Now you are going to transform those statements by shortening them and using action words. Your new description might come out like this: "Coordinate bid process. Identify vendors. Send bid forms. Track responses. Supervise filing and mailing staff."

You can do this for any responsibilities and for any jobs. It's not hard to do. Just use the action words list and cut out any unnecessary words. This has two important results. First, it makes your descriptions easy for prospective employers to read and to understand. Second, it commands attention. This is the kind of "no nonsense" approach that gets results.

ADDING "FACTS AND FIGURES"

Your last step in perfecting the descriptions of your work experience is to add "facts and figures." This is where you make your job or activity as concrete as possible. The questions to answer here are "How many?" "How much time?" "For whom?" "With what results?" There may be others that apply to your position. In the example we used above, we might add: "Contact approximately 250 vendors a year. Process bids in excess of $500,000 a year. File more than 2000 pages per year. Handle more than 30 phone calls a day for the purchasing department."

Again, you can do this for any job. It requires some estimating on your part, but no one knows your responsibilities better than you do. You will probably be surprised at the numbers you can add here. This information makes your job more "real" to prospective employers and makes you more appealing as a candidate. It is an extremely useful addition to your resume.

The three-part process you will use to fill out the "Work Experience" Worksheets is crucial for your resume. Be sure to finish all three steps for each "experience." There are three worksheets included at the end of this section. If you need more than three, photocopy the worksheet or use separate sheets of paper and follow the same process.

WORK EXPERIENCE WORKSHEET

Job title (or position held) _____

Employer (company, agency, etc.) _____

Dates: From_____ (month/year)

To _____ (month/year)

Briefly describe employer _____
_____

Responsibilities (Describe what you did in this job or activity. Put the most important responsibilities first if you can.)

1.

2.

3.

Add "action words." Restate each of the responsibilities you listed above, but make each statement as brief as possible and begin each with an action word.

1.

2.

3.

Add "facts and figures." You can either rewrite your statements from the section above with numbers, dollars, etc., or make a separate list.

1.

2.

3.

WORK EXPERIENCE WORKSHEET

Job title (or position held) _____

Employer (company, agency, etc.) _____

Dates: From_____ (month/year)

To _____ (month/year)

Briefly describe employer _____
_____

Responsibilities (Describe what you did in this job or activity. Put the most important responsibilities first if you can.)

1.

2.

3.

Add "action words." Restate each of the responsibilities you listed above, but make each statement as brief as possible and begin each with an action word.

1.

2.

3.

Add "facts and figures." You can either rewrite your statements from the section above with numbers, dollars, etc., or make a separate list.

1.

2.

3.

WORK EXPERIENCE WORKSHEET

Job title (or position held) _____

Employer (company, agency, etc.) _____

Dates: From_____ (month/year)

To _____ (month/year)

Briefly describe employer_____
_____

Responsibilities (Describe what you did in this job or activity. Put the most important responsibilities first if you can.)

1.

2.

3.

Add "action words." Restate each of the responsibilities you listed above, but make each statement as brief as possible and begin each with an action word.

1.

2.

3.

Add "facts and figures." You can either rewrite your statements from the section above with numbers, dollars, etc., or make a separate list.

1.

2.

3.

"ACTION WORDS"

To communicate quickly and powerfully with prospective employers, use "action" words wherever you can on your resume (and in your cover letter too). This list will provide you with suggestions, but it should not confine you. If you have a better word, use it. Take a look at the sample resumes at the back of the book to see how other job seekers have used "action words" in their resumes.

Developed	Initiated	Coordinated
Controlled	Advised	Authored
Performed	Implemented	Recommended
Designed	Maintained	Analyzed
Operated	Explained	Reviewed
Monitored	Suggested	Compiled
Generated	Adjusted	Produced
Revised	Created	Adapted
Supervised	Instructed	Planned
Enhanced	Built	Modified
Wrote	Reported	Determined
Debugged	Organized	Augmented
Conceived	Acquired	Purchased
Executed	Managed	Proposed
Assisted	Negotiated	Evaluated
Corresponded	Trained	Streamlined
Documented	Provided	Persuaded

Promoted	Improved	Examined
Simplified	Invented	Engineered
Arranged	Contacted	Packaged
Recognized	Programmed	Collected
Placed	Prepared	Saved
Investigated	Taught	Coached
Researched	Discovered	Counseled
Assembled	Constructed	Estimated
Installed	Repaired	Screened
Dispatched	Inspected	Audited
Budgeted	Cultivated	Tested
Appraised	Manufactured	Elicited
Lectured	Lobbied	Advertised
Interviewed	Hired	Fired
Logged	Catalogued	Copyrighted
Patented	Inventoried	Posted
Edited	Balance	Steered
Vended	Translated	Transcribed
Rescued	Displayed	Took part in
Closed (a deal)	Was in charge of	Was responsible for
Accomplished	Presented	Completed
Reorganized	Identified	Delivered

Restored	Instituted	Diagnosed
Sold	Made	Guided
Founded	Approved	Administered
Replaced	Increased	Established
Expanded	Calculated	Directed
Supplied	Produced	Headed
Interpreted	Represented	Scheduled
Distributed	Achieved	Conducted
Obtained	Selected	Referred
Formulated	Enlarged	Motivated
Devised	Solved	Studied
Ordered	Led	Consolidated
Eliminated	Decreased	Designated
Reduced	Processed	Composed
Served	Disproved	Detected
Won	Merged	

DALE'S RESUME REALLY DESCRIBES HIS CAREER IN THE
RESTAURANT BUSINESS.

4 ACCOMPLISHMENTS

DESCRIBING YOUR "ACHIEVEMENTS"

Completing the Accomplishments Worksheet will make you feel good. It focuses on your personal triumphs. Here's the idea. No matter what jobs or positions you have had, you have had some "accomplishments" along the way. These may be "big deal" accomplishments—like securing a new contract worth a million dollars to your company or starting up a new branch office by yourself—or they may seem like "no big deal" to you—like reorganizing a filing system or just getting everything done on time. This is the place to jot these down. Why? Because they show initiative on your part and an awareness of the needs of your employer. They show the *contributions* you have made in the past and they suggest the contributions you could make in the future. Remember, this is the kind of information that employers want but rarely find on resumes.

Staying with the example we used in the previous chapter, our assistant to the purchasing manager might fill out the Accomplishments Worksheet like this: "Streamlined purchasing process, saving the company time and paper. Started first computerized tracking process, making it possible to check the status of any vendor or bid. Found approximately 45 new vendors, resulting in savings of more than $25,000 in first year on the job."

As you can see, "action words" and "facts and figures" are as important on the Accomplishments Worksheet as they were on the "Work Experience" Worksheets. The sheets are set up in the same way and use the same three-step process. First, note your accomplishments. Second, add action words. Third, add facts and figures. Use the same experiences for your Accomplishments Worksheets that you used on your "Work Experience" Worksheets. Remember that these can be paid or unpaid jobs, part-time jobs, summer jobs, volunteer activities, internships, jobs in the home, etc. The focus here is on what you have achieved. Remember to be as specific as possible.

ACCOMPLISHMENTS WORKSHEET

Job title (or position held) _____

Accomplishments

1.

2.

3.

Add "action words." If you haven't already included action words, rewrite the statements above to be as brief as possible and begin each with an "action word."

1.

2.

3.

Add "facts and figures." If you haven't already included the specifics of your accomplishments, do so now. Rewrite each statement so that it includes numbers, dollars, etc.

1.

2.

3.

ACCOMPLISHMENTS WORKSHEET

Job title (or position held) _____

Accomplishments

1.

2.

3.

Add "action words." If you haven't already included action words, rewrite the statements above to be as brief as possible and begin each with an "action word."

1.

2.

3.

Add "facts and figures." If you haven't already included the specifics of your accomplishments, do so now. Rewrite each statement so that it includes numbers, dollars, etc.

1.

2.

3.

ACCOMPLISHMENTS

Job title (or position held) _____

Accomplishments

1.

2.

3.

Add "action words." If you haven't already included action words, rewrite the statements above to be as brief as possible and begin each with an "action word."

1.

2.

3.

Add "facts and figures." If you haven't already included the specifics of your accomplishments, do so now. Rewrite each statement so that it includes numbers, dollars, etc.

1.

2.

3.

5 | JOB SKILLS

DESCRIBING "ON THE JOB" SKILLS

The Job Skills Worksheets are the easiest worksheets yet. This is the place you can record your skills that are directly job-related.Even if you have never held a paying job, you have job skills. Again you have to "think like an employer" and identify skills that might be needed in the kinds of jobs you want. If you have gained any of those skills from the five activities that you have analyzed in the two previous chapters, include them on the appropriate Job Skills Worksheet. Here you can note the kinds of equipment you know how to operate or the computers and software packages you know how to use. Add skills here like your proficiency in speaking or writing languages other than English. Once again, use action words and be as concrete as possible.

Our purchasing assistant might record job skills like these: "Proficient in use of WordPerfect and Xywrite word processing software. Type 75 words per minute. Regularly use Lotus 1-2-3 spreadsheet software. Speak conversational Spanish. Often draft letters for supervisor." These are the kinds of skills you have too—and this is the spot to include them. Just as before, if you can't think of the kinds of job skills you have, take a look at your job description (if you have one), your on-the-job evaluations by your supervisor, or ask a colleague. Looking through the resumes in the back of this book can also help to stimulate your creativity.

Three Job Skills Worksheets follow. Use the same three experiences here that you have used on the "Work Experience" Worksheets and the Accomplishments Worksheets. Concentrate here on "what it takes to do this job," even if the job is part-time or unpaid. You have skills that you have learned or applied in every position you have held. This is the place where you can record them.

JOB SKILLS WORKSHEET

Job title (or position held) _____

What skills did you use in this position? What skills have you learned that are directly job related?

1.

2.

3.

Add action words. If possible, use action words in describing your skills. Rewrite each skill you listed above so that it is as direct as it can be.

1.

2.

3.

Add "facts and figures." If you haven't included specifics, now is the time to add them. Rewrite each skill so that it is as "fact filled" as possible.

1.

2.

3.

JOB SKILLS WORKSHEET

Job title (or position held) _____

What skills did you use in this position? What skills have you learned that are directly job related?

1.

2.

3.

Add action words. If possible, use action words in describing your skills. Rewrite each skill you listed above so that it is as direct as it can be.

1.

2.

3.

Add "facts and figures." If you haven't included specifics, now is the time to add them. Rewrite each skill so that it is as "fact filled" as possible.

1.

2.

3.

JOB SKILLS WORKSHEET

Job title (or position held) _____

What skills did you use in this position? What skills have you learned that are directly job related?

1.

2.

3.

Add action words. If possible, use action words in describing your skills. Rewrite each skill you listed above so that it is as direct as it can be.

1.

2.

3.

Add "facts and figures." If you haven't included specifics, now is the time to add them. Rewrite each skill so that it is as "fact filled" as possible.

1.

2.

3.

6 QUALIFICATIONS SUMMARY

A CAPSULE DESCRIPTION OF YOURSELF

Now that you know your personal skills, your personal qualifications, your experiences, your accomplishments, and your "job skills," this is a good time to try to summarize them. You are going to write a "capsule description" of who you are and what you have to offer to a prospective employer. This may become the opening section of your resume or it may be included in the cover letter that accompanies your resume. (With a few modifications, it might be used in both places.)

Your goal with the "qualifications summary" is to get an employer interested in you—interested enough to want to know more. This means that you need to "think like an employer." Think about what you have to offer. Think about what will appeal to a person who is screening resumes, looking for people who might be worth interviewing.

You have already done the work for this section. Take a look back through your worksheets and see what stands out to you. It's fine to steal from what you have already written. Your Skills Worksheet is a good place to start. Maybe you will find some key words in your Personal Qualifications Worksheet that show what you have to contribute. Perhaps you have some specific "work experiences" that should be highlighted so they can't be missed. Maybe it's an accomplishment that's so impressive it's bound to interest a prospective employer.

Just as you have done in your other worksheets, you should make sure that your summary uses brief, direct phrases and includes relevant "facts and figures." You might want to glance through the resumes at the back of the book to help formulate your description of yourself.

QUALIFICATIONS SUMMARY WORKSHEET

Who are you? What skills and qualifications do you have? What things do you want an employer to know about you? Use the spaces below to develop a brief summary of yourself.

QUALIFICATIONS SUMMARY: FIRST DRAFT

_____
_____
_____
_____
_____
_____
_____
_____

QUALIFICATIONS SUMMARY: SECOND DRAFT

_____
_____
_____
_____
_____
_____
_____
_____

QUALIFICATIONS SUMMARY: FINAL VERSION

_____
_____
_____
_____
_____
_____
_____
_____

7 EDUCATION

SUMMARIZING YOUR EDUCATION AND TRAINING

Employers are always interested in the education of their prospective employees. Their interest means that your resume will probably need a section that highlights your education. (There are a few exceptions to this rule that we will discuss when we bring all the pieces of the resume together, but for now you should assume that your resume will need to include your education and you should complete this section.)

The Education Worksheet that follows is pretty straightforward. You will be able to fill it out without a lot of effort. There are two identical sections for each level of your education, in case you attended more than one school or attained more than one degree at that level. This whole "building block" is fairly easy, so jump in and get started!

NOTE: IF YOUR FORMAL EDUCATION ENDED WITH HIGH SCHOOL, AND YOU HAVE BEEN OUT OF HIGH SCHOOL FOR MORE THAN FIVE YEARS, THE ONLY SECTIONS YOU NEED TO COMPLETE ARE THE LAST THREE: "VOCATIONAL OR TRADE SCHOOL," "WORK-RELATED COURSES," AND "TRAINING," IF ANY OF THESE APPLIES TO YOU.

EDUCATION WORKSHEET: HIGH SCHOOL

(NOTE: IF YOU COMPLETED TWO OR MORE YEARS OF COLLEGE, OR IF YOU ARE MORE THAN FIVE YEARS OUT OF HIGH SCHOOL, SKIP THIS SECTION.)

Name of high school _____

City and state _____

Attended from _____ to_____   Graduated _____

Grade point average _____   Rank in class _____

Honors, awards, prizes _____
_____

Special courses or programs _____

Extracurricular achievements _____

_____

Additional high school (if you attended more than one)

Name of high school _____

City and state _____

Attended from _____ to_____   Graduated _____

Grade point average _____   Rank in class (if known) _____

Honors, awards, prizes_____

Special courses or programs_____

Extracurricular achievements_____

_____

EDUCATION WORKSHEET: COLLEGE

Name of college _____

City and state _____

Attended from _____ to _____ Graduated _____

Grade point average _____ Rank in class _____

Degree _____ Major or concentration _____

Additional major or concentration _____

Honors, awards, prizes _____

Special courses or programs _____

Extracurricular achievements _____ _____

_____

Additional college (if you attended more than one)

Name of college _____

City and state _____

Attended from _____ to_____ Graduated _____

Grade point average _____ Rank in class _____

Degree _____ Major or concentration _____

Honors, awards, prizes _____

Special courses or programs _____

Extracurricular achievements _____

_____

EDUCATION WORKSHEET: GRADUATE SCHOOL

Name of graduate school _____

City and state _____

Attended from _____ to _____

Graduated _____

Grade point average _____ Rank in class _____

Degree _____ Field of study _____

Concentrations or specialties _____

Thesis or dissertation title _____

Honors, awards, prizes _____

_____

Special courses or programs _____

Extracurricular achievements _____

_____

ADDITIONAL GRADUATE SCHOOL (if you attended more than one)

Name of graduate school _____

City and state _____

Attended from _____ to_____   Graduated _____

Grade point average _____   Rank in class_____

Degree _____ Field of study _____

Concentrations or specialties _____

Thesis or dissertation title _____

Honors, awards, prizes _____

_____

Special courses or programs _____

Extracurricular achievements _____

_____

EDUCATION WORKSHEET: VOCATIONAL OR TRADE SCHOOL

Name of school _____

City and state _____

Attended from _____ to _____ Graduated _____

Diploma or certificate earned _____

Specialty or concentration _____

Grade point average _____ Rank in class _____

Honors, awards, prizes _____

Skills learned _____

_____

Additional vocational or trade school

Name of school _____

City and state _____

Attended from _____ to _____ Graduated _____

Diploma or certificate earned _____

Specialty or concentration _____

Grade point average_____ Rank in class _____

Honors, awards, prizes _____

Skills learned _____

_____

EDUCATION WORKSHEET: WORK-RELATED COURSES

List here any courses you have taken that are job-related. These can include short courses such as workshops and seminars and longer courses, either on-the-job or in educational institutions.

Course title _____

School name _____

City and state_____

Date course was taken _____

Diploma or certificate earned _____

Honors, awards, prizes _____

_____

Skills learned _____

_____

Additional Work-Related Courses

Course title _____

School name _____

School address (city and state) _____

Date course was taken _____

Diploma or certificate earned _____

Honors, awards, prizes _____

Skills learned _____

_____

EDUCATION WORKSHEET: TRAINING

If you have received special training, either on-the-job or in an educational institution, list it here.

Special training _____

School name _____

City and state _____

Dates of training: from _____ to _____

Diploma or certificate earned _____

Honors, awards, prizes _____

_____

Skills learned _____

_____

ADDITIONAL TRAINING

Special training _____

School name _____

City and state _____

Dates of training: from _____ to _____

Diploma or certificate earned _____

Honors, awards, prizes _____

Skills learned _____

_____

8 AWARDS

RECORDING RECOGNITION

Although you might think of "awards" as something won only at lavish banquets or internationally televised celebrations, the fact is that awards are handed out regularly for all kinds of achievements. Some are work related and some are not. Any award you have won might be listed on your resume. Ideally, the awards you include will be fairly recent (within, say, the last five years), and will communicate positively to a prospective employer (even an award for "good attendance" says something positive about you).

The Awards Worksheet lets you describe the awards you may have received. The decision to include an award on your resume is yours to make (and will be discussed further when we talk about the best ways to put your resume together). For now, put down on the worksheet any award that you are willing to discuss with a potential employer.

AWARDS WORKSHEET

Award received _____

Awarding organization _____

Date of award _____

Description of award _____
_____

Award received _____

Awarding organization _____

Date of award _____

Description of award _____
_____

Award received _____

Awarding organization _____

Date of award _____

Description of award _____
_____

Award received _____

Awarding organization _____

Date of award _____

Description of award _____
_____

9 MEMBERSHIPS

ASSOCIATIONS, CLUBS, AND ORGANIZATIONS

Your memberships in professional associations, clubs, organizations, and groups can be listed on your resume. They are most useful to you if they do any of the following: relate directly to the jobs you will be seeking; show your initiative outside your worklife—for example, a position of leadership in a volunteer role; or communicate something about you that you don't want to state directly in another part of your resume—perhaps your race, religion, ethnic background, or physical handicap.

Although your memberships can demonstrate positive qualities about you as a candidate for a job, they also offer prospective employers the chance to discriminate against you based on the stereotypes they have of the organizations you put on your resume. This is more obvious if you list an organization that usually includes only members of specific racial or religious groups, but it is true of other types of memberships as well. Remember to weigh these possibilities when you consider whether or not to include specific memberships on your resume.

Your memberships can be listed on your resume as simply the name of the organization or you can follow the name with the offices you have held, the number of years you have been a member, and even a brief description of the group itself if it is an association that is not well known. On the Memberships Worksheet, list the memberships that you consider to be the most important. For each, you can note any offices you have held or special projects you have coordinated. You can also include the length of your membership if you choose.

MEMBERSHIPS WORKSHEET

Name of organization _____

Number of years you have been a member _____

Offices held _____
(Add dates to each office if you think that these are important.)
_____
_____

Special projects (list your title if you held a position of leadership for the project)
_____
_____

Name of organization _____

Number of years you have been a member _____

Offices held _____
(Add dates to each office if you think that these are important.)
_____
_____

Special projects (list your title if you held a position of leadership for the project)
_____
_____

Name of organization _____

Number of years you have been a member _____

Offices held _____
(Add dates to each office if you think that these are important.)
_____
_____

Special projects (list your title if you held a position of leadership for the project)
_____
_____

10 PUBLICATIONS

YOUR WRITTEN WORDS

If you have written publications in the course of your work or schooling, you might want to list them in a special section of your resume. "Publications" can range from news notes printed in company newsletters to professional articles published in trade journals. If you have had your written words printed anywhere, they could be considered "publications."

You can arrange the Publications section of your resume with any structure you choose. (We will discuss this further when we describe how to assemble the resume.) The Publications Worksheet will help you organize the information you want to present. Some of your entries may contain more information than others. For now, put down all of the information that seems relevant. Note that there is space to include a description of your publication, even though this is not usually included on a resume. It's here in case you feel that the title and other information are not sufficient to describe your work. You don't have to use this section, but it's here if you need it. If you need additional worksheets, photocopy the worksheet or use a separate sheet of paper.

PUBLICATIONS WORKSHEET

Title (or brief description) of your writing_____
_____

Title (or brief description) of publication in which your writing was published
_____

Date of publication (include issue number if relevant) _____

Description of this work _____
_____

PUBLICATIONS WORKSHEET

Title (or brief description) of your writing_____
_____

Title (or brief description) of publication in which your writing was published
_____

Date of publication (include issue number if relevant) _____

Description of this work _____
_____

PUBLICATIONS WORKSHEET

Title (or brief description) of your writing_____
_____

Title (or brief description) of publication in which your writing was published
_____

Date of publication (include issue number if relevant) _____

Description of this work _____
_____

11 PERSONAL INFORMATION

USING INFORMATION TO YOUR ADVANTAGE

Once upon a time all resumes included a section that described what might be called "personal information." This section included things like marital status, number of children, church affiliation, health, etc. Today, it is against the law for employers to ask questions about race, religion, marital status, and physical handicaps (unless a handicap prevents accomplishing parts of a job). In some parts of the U.S. it is also illegal to ask about personal sexual preferences as well. And, although it is not illegal, it is considered improper for a prospective employer to ask any questions that are not directly job-related. As a consequence, "personal information" sections of resumes have largely disappeared.

However, there may be things about you that you would like an employer to know that simply don't fit into any of the categories we have covered. Examples are volunteer activities, leadership positions outside your worklife, a hobby that you are passionate about, a strong commitment to an organization or cause, etc. These can all be communicated on your resume under a heading like "personal information."

This same section can be used to relate information that an employer cannot ask, but that you may see as beneficial to your candidacy for a position. For example, if you are applying for a position where frequent out-of-town travel will be required, you might note on your resume: "Single, available to travel." (You can just as easily note that you are "Available to travel" without revealing your marital status.) Similarly, if you know that your race can be an asset in the job you are seeking, you could include it in "personal information" by stating it directly ("African-American" or "Native American," for example) or indirectly through your affiliations ("Member, Puerto Rican Action Organization").

The Personal Information Worksheet is completely optional. You don't have to fill in any information at all. If you think that there are facts about you that you would like a prospective employer to know, this is the place to include them. The topics below are only suggestions. Use the additional space at the bottom of the form to include any information that you think is important.

PERSONAL INFORMATION WORKSHEET

Social organization memberships _____
_____
_____
_____

Positions held in organizations _____
_____
_____
_____
_____

Hobbies _____
_____
_____
_____
_____

Awards or prizes for hobbies _____
_____
_____

Other information you might want to include on your resume _____
_____
_____
_____
_____
_____
_____
_____
_____

12 REFERENCES

WHAT THEY ARE AND HOW TO USE THEM

It is not required that you include in your resume a section entitled "References." However, you may want to put one in. "References" are people who can offer comments about you to a possible employer. Sometimes references are described as either "Work References" or "Character References" (also called "Personal References"). The first group would normally include former supervisors or co-workers who can evaluate your performance as an employee. The second group would include people who can offer an appraisal of your personal qualities. (Those in this group should not be relatives, but they can be longstanding friends.)

Most employers will want to speak with a previous employer before they offer you a job. (This is referred to as "checking references.") However, in most job fields it is not common for a prospective employer to check your references before interviewing you. Because of this, it is often more useful to have a separate printed list of your references available to hand (or mail) to an interested possible employer than it is to take up space on your resume listing information that it is not actually needed.

However, having just stated a rule, let's discuss the exceptions to it. First, if you are looking for work in a field where it is common for employers to check references before they interview candidates, you obviously need to include complete information about your references directly on your resume.

The second exception to the rule: if your references are well-known people, you may want to include them even if you are pretty sure that they won't be called before you are offered an interview. Including a person who is a "big name" reflects well on you and intrigues a prospective employer. If including references on your resume increases your chances of getting an interview, then definitely include references!

HANDLING REFERENCES

1) You can simply put down "References" as a heading and then say something like "Available on request." This is frequently encountered on resumes, but it doesn't have much real value. It implies that you do have references but, frankly, your prospective employer is going to expect this anyway.

2) You can use the general heading of "References" and list one to four people who could be contacted.

3) You can distinguish between "Work References" and "Personal References," including one or two people in each category.

REFERENCES RULES

1) Be sure to talk with your references before you put their names on your resume! You must have their permission before you include their names. They must be prepared to receive a call at any time and you must be confident that they will give your prospective employer an appropriate appraisal of you.

2) Be sure to include all of the information that a prospective employer might want to know: complete titles (even for your personal references), phone numbers if your references are willing to take phone calls, and the best time to call (if your references have expressed preferences).

3) Be sure that the information is accurate and up to date. It is embarrassing (and potentially damaging to your candidacy) to have the phone number of a reference listed incorrectly or to have the title of a reference be out of date.

The References Worksheet provides space for you to write down the information you need for each of your references. If you need additional space, photocopy the worksheet or use a separate piece of paper. Even if you have decided not to include references on your resume, you should complete the worksheet because you will still need to have a list of references available for prospective employers.

REFERENCES WORKSHEET: REFERENCE #1

Name _____

Title _____

Company/organization name _____

Address (use work address unless reference wants to be contacted at home)

_____

_____

Phone _____

Best hours to call _____

Relationship to you _____

REFERENCES WORKSHEET: REFERENCE #2

Name _____

Title _____

Company/organization name _____

Address (use work address unless reference wants to be contacted at home)

_____

_____

Phone _____

Best hours to call _____

Relationship to you _____

REFERENCES WORKSHEET: REFERENCE #3

Name _____

Title _____

Company/organization name _____

Address (use work address unless reference wants to be contacted at home)

_____

_____

Phone _____

Best hours to call _____

Relationship to you _____

REFERENCES WORKSHEET: REFERENCE #4

Name _____

Title _____

Company/organization name _____

Address (use work address unless reference wants to be contacted at home)

_____

_____

Phone _____

Best hours to call _____

Relationship to you _____

13 YOUR JOB OBJECTIVE

WHAT DO YOU WANT (AND WHAT CAN YOU CONTRIBUTE)?

You may have noticed that some resumes have a "job objective" right up at the top. Some don't. It's not essential that your resume have a job objective since you will almost always mail it with a cover letter (we'll get to the cover letter later). Even if you hand it directly to a person—and don't have a cover letter—it's likely that the person will know which position you are applying for and won't have to look at the "job objective" for a reminder.

The one situation in which it is useful to have a job objective is when your objective is an exact match with the job you are seeking. This makes you look like a contender right away. If you plan to look for only one kind of position, it makes sense to include a job objective in your resume. If you are going to be applying for a variety of positions, it makes more sense to include a "Qualifications Summary" (like the one you wrote earlier). We'll discuss this further when we talk about assembling your resume.

If you think that you will be applying for two or three different kinds of jobs and you plan to have a different resume for each type of job, then you might want to develop a separate job objective for each resume. For now, if you are going to look for only one kind of job, or if you will be applying for positions just like the one you have now, you should complete this section. If you will be looking for jobs that go by a variety of titles, skip this section altogether.

THE JOB OBJECTIVE WORKSHEET

Use the space provided on the Job Objective Worksheet to put your job objective into words. Try beginning with a phrase like this: "Seeking a position as..." or "Looking for a job in...." Be as specific as possible. If you find that you sound vague or general, abandon your efforts and be content with your "Qualifications Summary." For example, "Seeking a position as administrative assistant" is a good place to start if you know the title of the job you will be looking for. If you're not quite sure of the title, but you know the job field, you might consider an objective like "Looking for an entry-level job in advertising."

For a little more impact, you can add information about yourself. Try stealing a phrase or two from your "Qualifications Summary." For example: "Experienced administrative assistant, with three years of progressively responsible experience, seeks position where knowledge and skills can be applied." (Notice how this emphasizes experience, includes a number, and conveys the idea of serving an employer.) The inexperienced job seeker might try something like "Creative, hard-working young person seeks entry-level position in advertising."

MAKE A CONTRIBUTION

Remember that your job objective must make you look like the kind of employee who can make a contribution to a company or organization. The most common mistake made in writing job objectives is to focus on your own needs instead of focusing on the needs of your employer-to-be. Typical examples of this kind of mistake include phrases like these: "Seeking rewarding position..."; "Looking for a position that offers rapid advancement..."; "Seeking a job that allows relocation to Sunbelt region..."; "Looking for a position that promises financial compensation commensurate with my experience...," etc.

The emphasis in the statements above is all on the employee, not the employer. Frankly, the only people who care about the needs of the job seeker are the job seeker and the job seeker's family. If you can't write a job objective that makes you look immediately like the kind of worker someone would want to hire, stick with the "Qualifications Summary" and forget the "Job Objective."

Several of the sample resumes at the end of this book do include Job Objectives. You might want to look through the samples before you try to write your own.

JOB OBJECTIVE WORKSHEET

You may not get your job objective worded perfectly on your first try, or even on your second try. There is space below to try three times. An additional worksheet is available too—either to develop more job objectives for additional resumes or to keep rewriting your first one until it sounds perfect to you. Skim through the sample resumes at the back of the book for examples and inspiration.

JOB OBJECTIVE (First draft)

_____
_____
_____
_____
_____

JOB OBJECTIVE (Second draft)

_____
_____
_____
_____
_____

JOB OBJECTIVE (Final version)

_____
_____
_____
_____
_____

Questions to ask in evaluating your "job objective."

—Will my objective immediately position me as a qualified candidate for the positions I am seeking?

—Does it emphasize the contribution I can make to a company or organization?

—Will it interest an employer in reading further down the page?

JOB OBJECTIVE WORKSHEET

You may not get your job objective worded perfectly on your first try, or even on your second try. There is space below to try three times. Use this additional worksheet to develop more job objectives for additional resumes or to keep rewriting your first one until it sounds perfect to you. Feel free to skim through the sample resumes at the back of the book for examples and inspiration.

JOB OBJECTIVE (First draft)

_____

_____

_____

_____

_____

JOB OBJECTIVE (Second draft)

_____

_____

_____

_____

_____

JOB OBJECTIVE (Final version)

_____

_____

_____

_____

_____

Questions to ask in evaluating your "job objective."

—Will my objective immediately position me as a qualified candidate for the positions I am seeking?

—Does it emphasize the contribution I can make to a company or organization?

—Will it interest an employer in reading further down the page?

14 ELECTRONIC RESUMES

YOUR RESUME IN THE AGE OF COMPUTERS

Computers are being used just about everywhere these days, so it is no surprise to discover that they are changing the way that hiring is done at companies of all sizes. The reason is simple: computers can save time—and saving time saves money. By putting computers to work in the hiring process, employers are spending less and getting more. They are finding that computerized filing of resumes not only saves staff time but allows them to search through hundreds or thousands of resumes in a matter of a seconds to find candidates who meet their qualifications.

Only a few years ago, employers might have spent hours looking through stacks of resumes, reading each one as fast as they could. Today an employer can sit at a desk, enter the key qualifications of the ideal job candidate into a computer, and instantly receive a list of applicants whose resumes include the skills, experiences, accomplishments, and education that the employer wants.

Although this process may sound rather impersonal, and maybe a little intimidating, it is actually good news for job applicants. Once you know how to make your resume stand out in a computerized database, you have a better chance of being selected for an interview than you would have had in the old haphazard process of resumes piled up on someone's desk or stuffed into a file drawer in someone's office. And once your resume is in a company's computerized applicant tracking system, it is available to anyone in the company who is looking for a new employee. This means more job opportunities for you!

You might be wondering how you can make your resume attractive to a computer or how a computer can "read" your resume. That's exactly what you will find out in this chapter. Because it is very possible that your resume will end up in a computerized database, you owe it to yourself to read this chapter thoroughly and then evaluate your resume in light of what you have learned. You don't have to be a computer expert to design a resume that will appeal to a computerized search system. You just need a little knowledge of how these systems work to make them work for you. It may all sound kind of mysterious right now, but this chapter will eliminate the mystery.

What follows is a straightforward, simple-to-understand explanation of what can happen to your resume after you send it to a prospective employer—and what you can do to increase its chances of being seen after it arrives. The knowledge you gain in this chapter will make you a better-informed job seeker. The education you receive here will give you an advantage in today's job market.

WHAT HAPPENS TO YOUR RESUME ANYWAY?

Have you ever wondered what happens to your resume after you send it off to a potential employer? Do you think about how it is filed—and how it is retrieved? Have you ever received a letter that informs you that "your resume is being kept on file"? Did that letter make you speculate about how it would be found at some point in the future? Well, you're not alone. Most job applicants have had questions like these at one time or another.

In the days Before Computers ("B.C."), resumes were filed in filing cabinets. Probably they were kept in the Personnel Department (however large or small it was), and they sat there untouched until there was a job opening. When there was a position available, a department manager somewhere in the company made a phone call or sent a requisition form to Personnel describing the position and the qualifications of the kind of person who could fill it. Then it was someone's job to "see who's in the files." This person, who might have had a title like "Personnel Assistant" or "Recruiter," would go to the filing cabinets and take a look inside. He or she would select the resumes of people who looked like they met the specifications that the manager had set, would make a photocopy of the resumes, and would send them off to the manager who had requested them.

Actually, the process wasn't as efficient as it might sound from the description above. In reality, the resumes weren't organized very well and the person who looked through them had to spend a lot of time trying to find the resumes that matched the latest requisition. And the more resumes the company had on file, the more difficult it was to find specific ones when they were needed. Usually the best results that the Personnel Assistant could produce came from looking into the batches of resumes that had been collected the last time that a similar position had been available.

COMPUTERS ARE TODAY'S FILING CABINETS

With the help of computers, everything changed. Well, to be truthful about it, many things changed slowly over many years. Today, in companies that are using the capabilities offered by their computers, the same process of filing resumes and filling a job vacancy might look something like this. Now resumes are fed through an electronic scanner (more on this in a minute) and are "filed" in computers instead of in filing cabinets. Today's manager who needs a new employee still makes a phone call or sends a requisition form describing the positions and the ideal candidate to a department that is probably called Human Resources instead of Personnel, but something very different happens after that.

Instead of rooting around in file drawers looking for resumes, today's Human Resources Assistant sits down at a computer, inputs the requirements for the new employee and then watches the computer screen as a list of qualified candidates appears. Behind each of those names is a resume, which can be called instantly to the screen. After a quick appraisal from the person at the keyboard, these resumes are sent electronically to the computer of the manager who requested them. Whenever the manager has the time, he or she can look over the resumes and begin to invite candidates in for interviews.

Computers have revolutionized the ways in which resumes are stored and retrieved today. For the most part, file cabinets filled with resumes are a thing of the past. And although you can't be sure that the company that receives your resume will "file" it electronically, you have to assume that this is a definite possibility. That means that you have to understand exactly how computers can "read" your resume and match it up with job openings. Once you understand this, you can write a resume that is easy for a computer to read. And once you write a "computer friendly" resume, you will greatly increase the chances that yours will be one of the resumes that gets selected by that Human Resources Assistant who is looking for resumes to pass along to the manager who is ready to hire a new employee.

You're probably wondering how computers can take job descriptions from managers and find the resumes that are stored inside them. "How exactly do they do that?" you might be asking. It's a very good question—and the answer has a real impact on how you should construct your resume. To understand the answer, you have to know a little bit (but only a little) about how the words on your resume are filed in a computer. This is where "scanning" comes in.

SCANNING ALLOWS COMPUTERS TO "READ"

A "scanner" is a machine that "digitizes" the words and images on pieces of paper so that they can be used in a computer. Scanners are closely related to fax machines. Both make an electronic copy of a page of typed, written, or drawn words or images and then transmit that electronic copy. In the case of fax machines, they usually send the electronic copy to another fax machine. Scanners send the copy to a computer. Once it is in the computer, the information from the copy can be stored in a variety of ways so that it can be retrieved easily when it is needed.

Scanning isn't a foolproof process. Things can (and do) go wrong. If you have ever received a fax that is hard to read, you have seen the kinds of problems that scanners can have. Whole pages can sometimes look out of focus. Words can be "fuzzy" and individual letters can be broken up to the point where they are hard to decipher. And if you think that you have trouble reading a bad fax, you can imagine the problems that computers have. For all their celebrated intelligence, computers still can't think. They have to make do with "artificial intelligence" because they don't have brains. And they still have more trouble than humans do when it comes to making sense out of fuzzy letters and words.

The fact that scanners and computers are not excellent readers has some direct implications for your resume. Once you understand that their "reading" skills are limited, you can develop a resume that stands a better chance of being scanned successfully—that is, with as few errors as possible. The following tips will help you to produce a resume that is easy for scanners and computers to understand. In general, it pays to remember that you are a better reader than any piece of electronic gear. If your resume is difficult for you to read, it will be even more difficult for the hardware that is trying to make sense out of it for your prospective employer.

HOW TO CREATE A RESUME THAT A COMPUTER CAN "READ"

1. **Use a simple typeface**. Whether or not you do your own typing, you still have a choice of type styles for your resume. You want to select one that is "clean and simple." Your resume isn't the place to show off that bizarre new typeface you discovered that looks like it was drawn with chalk by a small child. This might get you noticed by the human who opens the envelope that holds your resume, but it is more likely to get your resume tossed into the nearest wastebasket than entered into the computerized applicant tracking systems that employers are using today.

Here's a quick lesson on typefaces. The styles that seem to have little "feet" at the bottom or little "hats" at the top of most of their letters are known as "serif" (pronounced "sare if") typefaces. Those without these little additions are known as "sans serif" (pronounced "sahns sare if") typefaces. Most computerized systems "read" sans serif typefaces better than they read serif faces. There is a smaller chance of running into problems if you use a sans-serif typeface. Samples of each are provided below so that you know what to look for when you are selecting a typeface yourself or specifying a face for someone else who is typing your resume. Also below you will find samples of two serif typefaces that are used frequently enough that they will probably be read successfully by most scanners.

This is a sample of a "serif" typeface. Note the "feet" and "hats" that some of the letters contain. These sometimes confuse scanners and computers.

This is a sample of a "sans-serif" typeface. Note that the letters in these words don't contain any decorations that might confuse a scanner or computer.

```
This is a sample of a typeface called Courier. Note how
closely it resembles the type that typewriters traditionally
used. Because it is so common, most scanners have been
programmed so that they can read this typeface.
```

This is a sample of a typeface called Helvetica. It has a long history and remains very popular—popular enough, in fact, that most scanners have been programmed so that they can read this typeface.

2. **Don't use tiny type**. Here's a simple rule of thumb: if the type on your resume is hard for you to read, it will be hard for a computer to "read." This means that if you have to strain to read your own resume, the scanner is going to have trouble translating your words for the computer. Don't take a chance. Use a type size that is clearly readable.

This is a sample of type that is too small. It is called "8 point" type.

This is a sample of type that is as small as most people (and most computers) can read easily. It is "10 point."

This is a sample of type that is easy to read. It could be used throughout a resume, if space allows. It is "12 point."

If you type your resume yourself or find someone to do it for you, be sure to specify a typeface that is at least "10 point" in size. This is a simple thing to do these days, and you will be happy that you were smart enough to attend to this detail. Type of this size is very likely to remain readable in all of the formats into which your resume might be put: faxed, electronically scanned, photocopied, and just read at a desk by a human (who will appreciate the fact that your resume doesn't cause undue eyestrain).

3. **Don't condense your type**. You might have noticed, perhaps in reading magazines or books, that type is sometimes set so that words almost run together on every line. This is because the type has been "condensed." The space between every letter has been reduced. You might be tempted to try this on your resume, so that you can fit more words onto a page. Don't give in to this temptation! Scanners are easily confused by condensed type.

This is an example of type that has been condensed. Note how the spaces between letters and words have been reduced.

This is an example of type that is normally spaced. Note how much easier it is to read.

Computerized typesetting systems can be adjusted to condense type, but be sure to tell your typesetter (whether it's another person or your own computer) to avoid condensing. (If you're looking for a phrase that communicates this to both humans and computers, try "Keep the type loose" and you'll have a good chance of getting the result you want.)

4. **Leave space between lines**. Another trick that is sometimes used to fit more type onto a page is to cut down on the amount of space between lines. Again, you might be tempted to try this trick on your resume, especially if you are trying to cram a lot of information into a small space. This is another temptation to avoid. Leaving out space between lines confuses scanners and invites trouble for your resume.

This is an example of what happens to the paragraph above when the space between lines is reduced:

Another trick that is sometimes used to fit more type onto a page is to cut down on the amount of space between lines. Again, you might be tempted to try this trick on your resume, especially if you are trying to cram a lot of information into a small space. This is another temptation to avoid. As with leaving out space between letters, leaving out space between lines confuses scanners and invites trouble for your resume.

If you want to be sure that you are giving the correct instructions to anyone who might be typing your resume for you, just say that you want "normal line spacing." Because computerized typesetting systems have to be specially adjusted to provide any setting other than "normal," you shouldn't have a problem here.

5. **Don't underline (or put in decorative lines).** Before the advent of computerized applicant tracking systems, it was common to find underlining used on resumes. Often it was used to emphasize important facts. Sometimes it was used in place of italic type, to set apart titles or names. Those days are gone! Today, underlining strains the capabilities of scanners and computers. They just don't understand the point of underlining. And if they don't understand it, they won't accept it. There's no reason to risk computer rejection by underlining anything in your resume.

In addition, while you're thinking like a computer, remember to leave out lines altogether. That means leaving out lines that serve a decorative function, like creating a border around the edge of your resume or putting a box around your name. You have to face the fact that computers don't like decorative lines (even if you do). When in doubt, leave them out.

6. **Use capital letters for emphasis.** Underlining is out, but capital letters are OK. Scanners and computers know how to "read" words that are written in capital letters. If you want to emphasize something in your resume, you can put it into capital letters. Of course, you're doing this only for the humans who will see your resume, since computers are not impressed by words that are written entirely in capitals. To a computer, a word is just a word.

7. **Boldface type "Yes"! Italic type "No"!** You have probably figured out by now that computers have limited "reading skills." That's because they have to be programmed to recognize every letter in every typeface that they are likely to encounter. As you can imagine, this programming is a massive task. Because it takes a lot of time, it's quite expensive. Although many typefaces are now easily understood, it's just too costly to try to program recognition of every available face. Since boldface type uses the same type styles as regular type (just a little "heavier" or "thicker"), computers generally manage quite well with it. However, italic type looks like a completely different set of characters, and computers are often baffled by it. You can see by the samples below why italic type is baffling. Use boldface type for emphasis, but skip italics altogether.

This is what boldface type looks like. It stands out nicely and is still easy to read.

This is what italic type looks like. You can see how confusing these slanted letters can be.

8. **Don't use graphics or ornaments.** In resumes that are designed for human eyes, one way to stand out from the crowd is to use some sort of ornamentation: maybe an unusual typeface for your name or starbursts next to your key qualifications. Perhaps you have emphasized certain parts of your resume with

asterisks or introduced them with "bullets." Unfortunately, when it comes to scanning your resume into a computer, these techniques backfire. Here is one place where you want your resume to "blend in with the crowd." It's only the words that count when computers are doing the reading.

9. **Don't "box" your type.** In the days before tracking systems, another way to highlight areas on a resume was to put a box around important words, or to put a band of gray behind them, or even to print the words in white in a band of solid black. That's not a useful technique today. Boxing and shading can be attractive to human eyes, but they're likely to overtax a scanner and computer. It's better to leave them out of your resume design.

10. **Be careful with abbreviations**. Abbreviations are tricky. Some are so common that every computer has been programmed to recognize them (like the two-letter codes that the U.S. Postal Service has assigned to identify every state). Some are common, but have a confusing array of presentations (is that basic college degree a BA, a B.A., an AB, an A.B., or a Bach. of Arts?). Others are specific to individual occupations (UNIX, VAX, MPX in the computer field for example). Still others are acronyms for professional associations, which can be perplexing too (does AMA stand for the American Medical Association or the American Marketing Association?). It's fine to use abbreviations on your resume, but you might want to spell out the full term too if you're not sure that a prospective employer (or an employer's computer) will know what the abbreviation stands for.

There is one more essential tip: DON'T PANIC! If you can't tell one typeface from another or if you can't tell the difference between boldface and italic type, don't worry. Try to follow the guidelines above but remember that computers don't work without humans to control them. Every company that scans your resume has a person sitting at the scanner whose job it is to look at each resume on the computer after it goes through the scanner. He or she gets paid to "clean up" that computerized resume so that it looks as much like the original resume as possible. Because these "verifiers" want to keep their jobs, they take their work seriously and try to eliminate as many mistakes as they can.

It's also true that technology is improving quickly. Scanning resumes and storing them in computers is a fairly new idea. The fact that it is also a good idea—one that promises to save money and increase efficiency for the companies that use it—means that a lot of effort is being put into this new technology. The scanning/storing process is constantly improving. Computers can "read" much better today than they could only two years ago. Next year they will be even smarter than they are today. All of this means that the chances of having your resume scanned successfully are increasing. However, you will still have an advantage over other job seekers if you pay attention to the guidelines above.

HOW RESUMES ARE RETRIEVED WHEN THEY'RE NEEDED

Now you know that "scanning" allows your resume to be electronically stored in computer databases (those "electronic filing cabinets" that are replacing the cabinets filled with paper resumes). You're probably wondering about the next part of this system. How do resumes get selected when there is a job available? Specifically, how is your resume found when you meet the qualifications for a position in a company that has your resume "on file" in its computer?

In most companies, supervisors still start the process that leads to retrieving resumes from computer databases. When they anticipate having a position available in their area, they tell someone in the Human Resources department (the department that used to be called "Personnel"). They usually do this on a requisition form of some sort—a form that asks relevant questions about the position itself and about the kinds of individuals who are most desirable as candidates to be interviewed. The supervisor is encouraged to describe both the job and the ideal candidates in detail, since this increases the chances of finding well-qualified people to interview.

When the Human Resources department receives the form, a human employee sits down in front of a computer and types in the key words and phrases from the manager's description and requests a list of candidates who meet the criteria the manager has provided.

"KEYWORDS" ARE THE KEY

Computers aren't really very smart. They can't actually think or reason. But, with decent programming, they can search through huge numbers of words and find exactly the ones that they have been told to find. Hunting through tens of thousands, or even millions, of words is something that computers can do with terrific speed and accuracy. This ability makes computers very well suited to find the resumes of job applicants in databases that contain hundreds or thousands of resumes. All they need to do their work is clear instruction. That's where those job requisitions come in. And that's what leads to the all-important "keywords."

The computerized search process isn't terribly complex. Basically, the computer is asked to find specific words or phrases or abbreviations that match those that were written on the requisition form by the supervisor who is looking for a new employee. To make the search process more efficient, and therefore faster, the requirements might have been put into 'fields" like Level of Education, Certification, Experience, etc. But, fundamentally, the computer is looking for words. And looking for words is something that computers do very well (and very quickly). The words and phrases and abbreviations that they search for are called "keywords."

If you think about it for a minute, you can see that the more closely the words and phrases on your resume match the keywords of the computer's search, the greater the odds are that your resume will selected. And if you think about it for another minute, you'll realize that you can definitely improve your chances if you use the same keywords in your resume that the computer will use in its hunt. But, you might be asking, how can I know what keywords the computer will be trying to find? And how can I make sure I use the same keywords in my resume? Take a look at the tips below!

PUTTING "KEYWORDS" TO WORK FOR YOU

Since keywords are crucial to your success in computerized applicant tracking systems, it is essential that they appear in your resume. The good news is that many of them are probably there already, if you have written a resume. More good news is that it won't take extraordinary efforts on your part to pack your resume full of them, even if you have never written a resume before. Here are some suggestions on how to include these vital keywords in your resume.

1. **If you have a job description, use it!** If you are applying for a specific position, and you have a description of the position, you possess many of the keywords already! That job description, whether it comes from a newspaper ad, a letter from a friend, or directly from the Human Resources Department, is a goldmine. It is very likely to use many of the keywords that will later be entered into a computer when the electronic search for candidates is conducted. Since your resume will be scanned exactly as you write it, make sure that you include as many keywords as you can!

If the job description includes the phrase "Bachelor's degree required," be sure to use the phrase "Bachelor's degree" in your resume (although you should also include the same information in other ways too, just in case the computer is told to search differently). In this case, your resume might say: "Bachelor's degree in English. B.A., University of Texas." If the job description uses abbreviations, use the same abbreviations in your resume (but, again, spell out the full name if you think that the computer search might be conducted using the full name).

For example, if the job description says "Must be familiar with TQM," your resume might state: "Familiar with TQM (Total Quality Management)." If there are specific product names in the job description, include those same names in your resume.

Here's one example from a job description: "Requires knowledge of WordPerfect, Word for Windows, and Lotus." You would want to include the identical phrase in your resume: "Knowledge of WordPerfect, Word for Windows, and Lotus." You could then go on to list other software packages that you know how to use, but you will have included the keywords exactly as they were written in the description.

2. **If you don't have a job description, "think like an employer."** You may not have an exact job description, but you obviously know a few things about any job for which you are submitting a resume. Before you develop your resume, spend a few minutes listing the key requirements of the job you hope to get. Be as specific as possible. Do you have to type a certain number of words per minute (wpm)? Is certification required? Do you need a college degree? To make your list, "think like an employer." What is your future employer likely to be looking for in an employee? You might go so far as to write out a job description yourself, and then write a resume that responds directly to that description—including the keywords!

Remember, too, that job descriptions are usually available from the company that has a job opening. All you have to do is ask for one. If you don't know where to start, contact the Human Resources or Personnel department. If you need it in a hurry, ask if they can fax it to you—or stop in and pick up a copy. It's definitely worth the effort!

3. **Learn the "keywords" in your field and use them in your resume!** Every occupation has its "buzzwords," abbreviations, and acronyms. If you think about it, you probably know lots of them that are specific to the type of work you do (or want to do). These are "keywords" and they need to be included in your resume. It will pay off to make a list of these before you start writing a resume.

If you don't know the field very well, there are at least two steps that you might want to take: 1) talk to someone who is already employed and is likely to know the jargon; and 2) take a look at advertisements for available jobs. Your task here is simple: you want to find out what the keywords are. You want to know which words are going to turn up on that requisition form (the one that starts the electronic search process), so that you can use those same words on your resume.

WHAT HAPPENS WHEN THE COMPUTER SELECTS YOUR RESUME?

Computerized applicant tracking systems are designed not only to store and retrieve resumes, but also to send resumes directly to the managers who have requested them. As you have probably guessed, the computerized keyword search produces a list of candidates who meet the search criteria. The person who is conducting the computerized search then looks at the electronically-stored resume of each candidate to verify that he or she does, in fact, have the necessary background and qualifications to fill the available position. Next, the electronic resumes are forwarded to the manager who will select the candidates to be interviewed. They can be printed out in their entirety and passed along on paper, or they can be sent electronically so that they are available on the manager's computer when he or she is ready to look them over.

Of course, you want to be selected by the computer AND by the manager who will be doing the interviewing for the job. This means that your resume has to be written with both the computer and the manager in mind. It has to observe all of the rules for scanning success that were spelled out earlier in this chapter. It has to include "keywords" that are likely to be used in the computerized search process. And, finally, it has to present you in an appealing way to a manager who may see your resume only on a computer screen!

HOW TO ENSURE SUCCESS WITH COMPUTERS

In addition to the tips noted above, there are a few more ways to ensure that your resume will be able to be successfully scanned and entered into a computerized resume storage system. These are each simple steps that you can take when you create your own resume. If there is a chance that your resume will be entered into a computer, then you should use each of the tips below when you develop your resume. It only takes a little attention to detail. In the long run, you will be glad you paid attention!

1. **Use white paper**. Although some light colors of paper don't confuse the scanner, why take a chance? Use black type on white paper and you will give your resume the best odds of being easily scanned.

2. **Use standard size paper, printed on one side.** Although it's true that the computer doesn't care how long your resume is, the scanner cares how long your paper is. It is set up to scan 8 1/2" X 11" paper and that is how your resume should be submitted.

3. **Use type that is large enough to read easily**. If you can't read your own resume easily, a scanner probably can't read it either! Remember that "10-point type" is as small as you should use on your resume.

4. **Use a laser printer**. In the chapter on printing your resume, you will hear more about your options, but if you are using a computer to produce your own resume, be sure to use a laser printer. The type that is reproduced by a dot matrix printer is made up of many little dots (instead of complete letters) and the image quality is not good enough to be scanned with 100% accuracy. If you have someone else type your resume, be sure the final output is done on a laser printer.

5. **Don't use graphics of any kind**. Remember that scanners are only able to "read" type. Anything other than words will confuse them. To ensure scanning success, your resume should not contain borders (even simple line borders), boxes, designs, pictures, or background images behind type.

6. **Put your name in the upper left corner.** Although it's true that the person who "verifies" your resume after it is scanned will be sure that your name and address show up on the electronically-stored copy of your resume, it is still helpful to put your name and address in the top left corner of your resume. Scanners are usually programmed to "look" for your name here.

7. **Be sure to include "keywords."** As you learned above, "keywords" are the keys to success in a computerized search. Once you know the keywords in your field, be sure that they show up on your resume. If you are applying for a specific position and have a job description, it is worth rewriting your resume to be sure that the words and phrases used in the job description are also used on your resume.

8. **Don't fax your resume**. Since you know that there is a chance, with almost any available job, that your resume will be scanned and stored in a computer, don't take chances. Don't fax it unless you have to (and, if you do fax a resume, follow up by sending a paper copy too). There are many reasons why a fax can be "degraded" during transmission, but the point is that a faxed copy is never as good as the original. And scanning a faxed copy is never as good as scanning an original. Some day it may be possible to fax directly to a scanner, and avoid the paper copy altogether, but that day hasn't arrived yet.

9. **Don't fold your resume**. The resume you provide is the resume that will get scanned. If it is folded, it is quite possible that it will give the scanner problems. If the fold lines run across your lines of type, the letters on those lines are more difficult for the scanner to decipher clearly. What's the solution? Use an envelope that is large enough to contain your resume without folding. Envelopes that are 9" x 12" are readily available at stationery stores.

10. **Don't worry**. Once you have followed all of the advice in this chapter, you can take a deep, relaxing breath. You have done all you can. The computer programs that make sense out of electronically scanned text are continually becoming more sophisticated. If your prospective employer encounters difficulties entering your resume into an applicant tracking system, you might receive a phone call or note asking you to clarify certain information on your resume. This will alert you to changes you should make before you send out your resume again.

There is an acronym from the computer industry that is worth considering when you are developing your resume: "GIGO." It stands for "garbage in = garbage out." If your resume is disorganized, difficult to read, filled with misspellings, or just plain unimpressive, it won't get any better (or any more impressive) when it is scanned into a computer! If your resume doesn't represent you well on paper, it won't represent you well on a computer screen. You have a head start on other job seekers who haven't read this book and don't know about computerized applicant tracking systems and their electronically scanned resume storage and retrieval capabilities. But you still have to develop a resume that "sells" you to your prospective employers. If you have paid attention to the suggestions in previous chapters and if you have incorporated the advice in this chapter into your resume, you will have a resume that will get the attention of both humans and computers!

HOW TO SEND YOUR RESUME BY ELECTRONIC MAIL

As computers become more widely used in all aspects of the job application process, you may be asked to send your resume to a prospective employer by "e-mail." If you have prepared a "scannable" resume following the guidelines in this chapter, it won't be difficult for you to e-mail it when you are asked. Often the request will be accompanied by instructions, but here are a couple of tips that you might not receive.

First, you will have to have your resume stored on the computer from which the e-mail is sent and your e-mail will have to be able to send documents (usually called "attachments"). Second, your resume will need to be stripped of all of its "formatting codes." These are the codes that are inserted by your word processing software to show where paragraphs begin or to identify boldface type, for example. Most word processing packages include the option of removing these codes. Check the on-line "help" feature or the documentation booklet for your software. You can also ask a more computer literate colleague or friend for assistance. One "buzz phrase" to use is "converting a text file to ASCII." This is a phrase you can look up in your "help" file or use when you ask a person for assistance.

Remember when you e-mail your resume that is simply a collection of words. It doesn't actually look like a resume. This puts a greater emphasis on the words you have chosen to use. Specifically, it highlights the importance of "keywords." If you are applying for a specific position and have seen an advertisement or job description for the position, be sure to include exact words and phrases in your resume (assuming that you are being truthful of course). The more precisely your qualifications match those of the ideal candidate, the greater are the chances that a computerized search will find your resume. And having your resume selected is the first step toward getting the job!

"KEYWORDS": YOUR KEY TO SUCCESS

The concept of keywords is simple. Basically, keywords are the words or phrases used in searching any database of candidates. They are the words or phrases that are entered into a computer to find applicants. They provide a means of "matching" available candidates with available jobs. Obviously, these words are important to job seekers. Keywords can make the difference between being selected or ignored for a job opening.

How can you put keywords to work for you? Actually it's not hard to do. If you have a description of the specific job you want (or a description of the general type of job you want), you probably already know some keywords. Even if you have a job description from an advertisement, it's likely that you know some keywords, because it's likely that they appear right there.

Because nearly every word or phrase in a job description is a potential keyword, you need to pay very close attention to the wording of job descriptions (yes, even those that appear in classified ads). To maximize your chances of being selected by the computer search, you need to include those words and phrases in your resume or application EXACTLY AS THEY APPEAR IN THE DESCRIPTION. If an ad uses the phrase "three years of experience," then your resume should use the same phrase. If a job description notes that a "B.S. Degree in Biology" is required, your resume should contain the same phrase.

It is important for you to have your own list of keywords to use when you prepare your resume. Many of these words and phrases already appear on your previous worksheets. They might be called "personal qualifications," or "accomplishments," or "skills," or they might be included on your "work experience" worksheets. On the "Keywords Worksheet" that follows, you can note specific words and phrases that you think must be included in your resume. Once you have your personalized list, all you have to do is include these on your resume. So take a few minutes right now to complete the worksheet that follows.

"KEYWORDS" WORKSHEET

JOB TITLE _____

SKILLS KEYWORDS_____

_____

_____

_____

EXPERIENCE KEYWORDS _____

_____

_____

_____

EDUCATION KEYWORDS _____

_____

_____

_____

TECHNICAL KEYWORDS_____

_____

_____

_____

MISCELLANEOUS KEYWORDS _____

_____

_____

_____

Congratulations! You are ready to start putting your resume together! Just follow the suggestions in the chapter ahead and you will be able to produce the resume that is right for you—the kind of resume that gets jobs.

15 ASSEMBLING YOUR RESUME

PUTTING IT ALL TOGETHER!

Good news! Now that you have created each of the components of your resume, all you have to do is assemble them and your resume will be complete! Since you have all of the pieces, you can assemble your resume in exactly the way you choose. This approach allows you to create one resume to use throughout your job search or to design a "customized" resume every time you need a resume.

You probably have a specific job in your mind right now. If you don't have a job in mind, you probably know the type of work you will be looking for. Think about your job goals as you put together your resume.

You don't have to use everything you have written so far. There may be items on your worksheets that you want to leave off your resume altogether. There may be entire worksheets that you don't want to include. These are your decisions.

There are very few strict rules to follow in creating a resume. There is not one "right way" to do it. Everything that follows is good advice, but it is not rigid. Remember that your objective is to design a resume that will get you an interview. Nobody knows your strengths and capabilities better than you do. Here is your opportunity to tell your next employer exactly what you can contribute. Hold that thought, and let's get started putting your resume together.

HEADING

Start your resume with your name, address, and phone number at the top of the page. Since prospective employers are likely to call during the day, try to provide a phone number where you can be reached during regular business hours. If that is not possible for you, use a number where a message can be left for you. (You may want to consider purchasing or borrowing an answering machine, contracting with an answering service for the duration of your job search, or securing an electronic "mail box" from your local phone company.) If you simply cannot be contacted during normal working hours, note next to your phone number the hours that are best to reach you. (Take a look at the sample resumes to see how others handle this.) If you have a fax number that prospective employers can use to contact you, include this under your phone number.

NOTE: It is not necessary to label your resume with the word "Resume." The people who receive your resume will know what it is.

JOB OBJECTIVE

As we discussed in the section on writing a job objective, it is not necessary to have an objective on your resume. Only when your job objective matches the position you are applying for does the job objective really "work." The problem with having an objective that doesn't correspond directly with your target job is that it looks as if you prepared your resume with a different job in mind. This may raise concerns in the mind of your prospective employer from the start.

If you are planning to look for work in only one field and you have prepared a job objective that is relevant to that field, feel free to use it at the beginning of your resume. If you are able to prepare a new resume each time you apply for a new job, you can modify your job objective so that it exactly matches the job. Otherwise, you might consider a "Qualifications Summary" instead (you have already prepared this on an earlier worksheet).

There isn't much point in vague job objectives like "Seeking a position that utilizes my talents" or "Want a challenging position in which I can apply my skills." Remember that employers want to know what you can do for them. Your personal goals aren't all that important here. Avoid saying what you hope to get from a job and focus on what you have to contribute!

QUALIFICATIONS SUMMARY

After you completed your skills, personal qualifications, "work experience," accomplishments, and job skills worksheets, you compiled a summary of your qualifications—the qualities that make you an asset to an employer. You might begin your resume with this "Qualifications Summary." Look back at it now and evaluate it as a way to start off your resume. Does it communicate to a potential employer your skills, personal qualifications, or experience in a way that makes you look like a person who could make a contribution to an employer? If the answer is "yes," consider starting your resume with this statement. You could call it "Qualifications" or "Summary," or you could make up your own category. You might also include it with no heading at all. Because it is at the top of your resume, it will be seen (and read) by everyone. It is the perfect place to "introduce" yourself to a possible employer.

YOUR GREATEST ASSETS

After you have stated your job objective or provided a summary of your qualifications, it's time to put forth your strongest qualifications for the jobs you want. These will be different for each resume writer. Fortunately, all you have to do is choose from what you have already written. Look back over your skills worksheets, your personal qualifications worksheets, your accomplishments worksheets, your experience worksheets, and your education worksheets. Which one set is likely to be most important to your prospective employers?

Traditionally, resume writers have concentrated on their experiences, but this has not always served them well. If your experience isn't very extensive, or isn't very impressive, why give it such a prominent position in your resume? Your skills, qualifications, or accomplishments might give your resume a much better start. It is often better to begin with one of these anyway, since employers will always continue to read down your resume until they find your experience and your education. Knowing that, you can save these two categories until the end of your resume if they are not your greatest assets.

Here are some guidelines to follow. Keep in mind that these are only suggestions. Your goal is to present your qualifications in the order you think is right for you. You get to decide how you are going to present yourself on paper to possible employers.

Guidelines for Great Assets

1. Experience: If you are looking for a job that is closely related to previous jobs you have held, consider putting your experience first.

2. Accomplishments: If you have some impressive accomplishments to your credit (whether they are work-related or not), you might want to list these first, just to get the reader's attention. If they arouse curiosity about you, they will keep the reader reading.

3. Education: If you have recently graduated from college or have recently acquired a degree, diploma, or certificate that is directly related to the work you are seeking, think about stating that right at the beginning. This is especially true if you don't feel that you have impressive skills, qualifications, accomplishments, or experience.

If you are presently enrolled in an educational program that is directly related to the job you are hoping to obtain, you can treat this just as if you already had a certificate or degree. Just note that you are "presently enrolled" and then list the type of program, the subjects or courses, honors or awards, and other information that is relevant to an employer. If you are attending school while you are working (even if you are taking courses without formal enrollment in a program), include that fact on your resume.

If you do put your education first, try to include a mention of particularly important classes, your grade point average (if it is higher than a "B"), your class rank (if it is in the top 20% or so), and other facts that highlight your educational achievements. See the sample resumes for examples of how others have handled this.

4. Skills: If you have a skills list that is especially appealing to a prospective employer (and you probably do), it is always a good way to begin. You want your skills list to arouse enough interest to keep a prospective employer reading your resume. Most lists draw a reaction something like this: "These skills look like ones we could use." If yours can get a similar response, put your skills list first.

5. Personal qualifications: Even if you don't think that you have a great deal to offer, you do have your personal qualifications. These are definitely an asset; they are uniquely yours; and they are a fine place to start a resume. Maybe you are looking for your first job; maybe you are returning to work after a long absence; or maybe you are changing careers to an area in which you have no previous experience. Your personal qualifications may be the perfect place to begin.

As you will see on the sample resumes, you don't have to call your personal assets "personal qualifications." You can title this section "Profile," or "Strengths," or "Skills," or "Expertise"—or you can make up any other heading you like.

The point is to draw attention to your strengths as a candidate, whatever they may be.

MORE ASSETS

Once you have selected the section that you think presents you most favorably to a possible employer, you can let the other sections fall into place below that one. Look over your worksheets for experience, skills, qualifications, accomplishments, and education. Decide whether there are any you want to leave out altogether, and then put the rest into the order that best presents your strengths. Remember that employers are likely to keep reading until they find your experience and your education, so put those after your skills, qualifications, and accomplishments, unless they are more important than the other possible sections.

AWARDS, MEMBERSHIPS, PUBLICATIONS

After you have included all of the information listed under "More Assets" above, it's time to take a look at the rest of your worksheets and put them into the order of their importance. If you have completed these worksheets, take a look at them now and decide how you would like to order them in your resume. You don't have to include them at all, but try to work them into this first draft. You can see how you like them later.

PERSONAL INFORMATION

Including any personal information on your resume is entirely optional. You are not obligated to include this information. However, if you feel that it is a boost to your candidacy for a position, this is the place to include it.

REFERENCES

Look back at the references worksheet you prepared. If you want to include your references—the names, titles, addresses, and phone numbers of people who can tell potential employers about you—they should go at the end of your resume. If you are not planning to put names in your resume, you can either leave the "references" section out altogether or you can include a line that says "References available on request."

CONFIDENTIALITY

There are many reasons that job-seekers may want their resumes kept confidential. The most obvious reason, of course, is that they don't want a present employer to know that they are looking for another job. If you ask that your application for a position (or even your inquiry about the availability of a position) be kept confidential, your request will usually be honored. If you do want your resume to be considered a confidential document, you should state that on the resume itself.

Although you can put a note at the top of the first page of your resume that states "CONFIDENTIAL RESUME," it is more common to include a note at the end of your resume. It can have a heading of its own (like "Education" or "References"), but it doesn't have to be this prominent. A clear note at the bottom of your resume can be sufficient. It might state: "This resume is submitted in confidence. Please keep confidential." It can address a specific concern: "Please do not contact present employer." Or it can be a simple declaration: "Please respect the confidentiality of this resume."

16 PRINTING YOUR RESUME

HOW TO GET THE BEST RESULTS

The appearance of your resume is important. Because your resume will usually be compared with many others, it needs to be competitive. This doesn't mean that you must use dramatic graphics or arresting typefaces, but it does mean that you need to pay attention to what your resume looks like. You have put a lot of time and energy into the words that make up your resume, and it is worth putting a little more time and attention into its appearance.

WORD PROCESSING

Whatever appearance you have in mind for your resume, your first step is to have it typed on a word processor. You can do this directly from the worksheets you have prepared in earlier sections of this book or you can write out a version by hand that puts everything in exactly the order you want. If you have access to a word processor, and you are a decent typist, you can enter all of your information yourself. If you aren't able to use a word processor, you might know someone who can help you out. If you don't have a friend—or a friend of a friend—who can enter your resume into a word processor, you can turn to a typing, word processing, or secretarial service in your community. You can find this kind of help in your local telephone directory.

It might take a couple of tries to get everything to look just right and to fit properly. You will probably have to do some editing to get the material from your worksheets into the format you want. You will also need to do some proofreading to check for spelling mistakes. Most word processing systems have built-in "spelling checkers" that can check the spelling once the resume has been typed, but you will still need to check the overall accuracy. If you are not a good speller or proofreader, get some help from someone who is. If you have used a professional service, it should be able to provide help with this checking.

All of the entering of information into the word processor is known as "inputting." You are putting information in. The next stage is the "outputting," or printing. Whether you do the typing yourself or have someone do it for you, you will do your proofreading on the "output"—a printed piece of paper (also known in computer-speak as "hard copy"). The printer may be able to produce a very professional-looking printed copy, or it may only be able to turn out a copy that is decent enough for proofreading but not good enough to actually call your resume.

Some printers that are hooked up to word processors are able to produce different typefaces, and in different sizes as well. You or your typist can manipulate the appearance of the type on the page to get just the look you want. You will find a variety of resumes in the sample pages that follow. You might want to choose one or more that really appeal to you so that you can use them as models when you prepare your own. If you or your typist can produce a printed copy that satisfies you, you can skip the next paragraph and go directly to the section below entitled "Printing vs. Photocopying."

If you do not have access to a printer that can give you the kind of printed version you want, you still have options available. If you can get a diskette (a "floppy disk") from the word processor, you should be able to take it to a business in your community that has the kind of printer you need to produce the resume you want. Again, you might take samples from this book to show to the person who will be formatting the output to get the results you are looking for. If you don't know where to turn for a high-quality printout of your resume, check your local telephone directory under headings like "typesetting," "desktop publishing," or "printing." Often these same businesses can help you get your resume printed or copied as well (see below).

PRINTING VS. PHOTOCOPYING

Once you have one copy of your completed resume, you can have additional copies printed or photocopied. Photocopying is cheaper and faster and can often produce excellent copies. Professional printing will always produce outstanding copies (if your original is outstanding), but it may not be worth the extra expense to you.

Generally, if you are planning to have fewer than 100 copies made, you should turn to a photocopying service that uses high-speed, high-quality copy machines. Photocopies cost only a few cents apiece and should look nearly as good as your original. Copy services offer a choice of papers, sometimes with matching envelopes (see the next section for more information on paper selection), and they can often do the copying while you wait. You can also ask to see what a copy will look like on different papers and—for a very small charge—the copy service will run these for you so that you can decide which you like best. If you are not sure where you can find a copy service, check your local telephone directory under such headings as "photocopying" or "copying and duplicating services."

If you are planning to have more than 100 copies made, you can still use a photocopying service, but you might also investigate offset printing as well. There are at least three reasons to consider using a printing service instead of a copying service:

1) You have designed a resume that will be difficult to reproduce well on a photocopier, because of the typefaces you have selected or the surface texture of the paper you want to use (photocopying works better on smooth papers than on textured papers);

2) You work in a field that values appearances highly (graphic arts, fine arts, or any design-related field, for example);

3) You are seeking a high-level position (middle manager or above), in which other applicants are likely to have well-designed and printed resumes.

Fortunately, printers frequently offer a range of printing services and can usually advise you on the type of printing that will best meet your needs. Take your original with you to a commercial printer, tell the printer how many copies you need and the kind of paper you want to use, and ask for advice. In one shop these days you may find both copying and printing services. If you don't know of a printing service in your community, check your telephone directory under such headings as "printers" or "copying and duplicating services."

PAPER SELECTION

The paper you select for your resume is not vital to the success of the resume. Resumes that are cleanly printed on plain white paper and meet all of the criteria outlined on the "Resume Tips" (Chapter 18) can be just as well received by potential employers as those that are printed on colored and textured paper and arrive in matching envelopes, with cover letters computer-printed on matching paper. However, it is true that employers receive many resumes, especially for advertised positions. Even though they try to select candidates to interview based on what is on the paper (and not the paper itself), it is hard not to be influenced by appearances. This is especially true in businesses where appearances are an important part of the work, such as design and art-related enterprises, architecture, interior decorating, and similar ventures.

Generally speaking, it costs very little more money to have your resume copied or printed onto colored paper than onto white paper. Some copy services and printers stock envelopes to match selected papers, and all will be happy to sell you extra sheets of the paper you select for your resume so that you can use matching paper for your cover letters. Ask to see available papers and ask directly about the comparative costs before you make your selection.

KEEP COLOR CONSERVATIVE

As far as color is concerned, keep it conservative unless you know that you will be looking for work in a job field that values creativity. In most fields it is fine to stand out a little in a pile of resumes, but it is not OK to stand out a lot. Off-white paper colors and so-called "neutrals" are safe choices if you want to move away from white. These may have names like "cream," "tan," "buff," "ivory," etc. Very pale shades of blue or gray are also fine. If you are in doubt about a color, stay with a light one.

There are several other reasons to stay with a light-colored paper that has very little texture to it (in other words, a "smooth-finish" paper). First, it is likely that your resume will be photocopied after it is received by a prospective employer, and light colors photocopy better than dark colors.

The second reason to keep the paper color light (and the ink dark) is the likelihood that you or an employer will fax your resume and you will want the fax to transmit as cleanly as possible.

A third reason to keep the paper light and smooth is the growing use of "scanners." These machines optically "scan" your resume to put it into a computerized database.Once scanned, a resume can be assigned to various headings under which it can be "filed" and transmitted electronically to selected employees throughout the corporation (and around the world). Like copiers and fax machines, scanners produce their best results when there is the greatest contrast between paper and ink.

ENVELOPE SELECTION

For your cover letters, it is a nice touch—but certainly not necessary—to use paper that matches the paper of your resume. You can purchase extra sheets inexpensively when you have your resume printed and you can type your cover letters directly on these sheets (or put the sheets into the printer for your word processor). Again, this is not essential. It is just another way to make you look attractive as a job candidate, and you should take advantage of the opportunity if you can.

It is not essential that you have matching envelopes (since your envelope is likely to be tossed out as soon as it is opened), so this is one place where you can save some money. You also don't need to have envelopes printed with your name and address. This is expensive and not usually necessary (unless you are looking for a very high-level job). However, it is important that your envelopes be typed and not handwritten if this is possible for you to do.

One investment that is worth considering (and it is a small additional expense) is the purchase of envelopes that are larger than standard business envelopes. The standard envelope requires you to fold your resume and cover letter twice to fit it into the envelope. A larger, 5" x 7" envelope requires only one fold, and the still-larger 9" x 12" envelope allows you to insert both cover letter and resume without a fold at all.

The larger sizes also make your resume stand out in the mail and may help your envelope be opened before others. But it is the fold lines that are the most important reason to think about using a large envelope. As discussed in the section on paper selection, there is a good chance that your resume will be photocopied, faxed, or scanned after it is received by an employer. All of these processes work better when the "original" is a flat, unfolded piece of paper. The extra effort you make to ensure that your resume (and cover letter) arrive in great condition may pay off for you in ways that you can only anticipate now. It's worth a thought on your part.

CUSTOMIZED RESUMES

Just as cover letters need to be individualized every time you send out your resume, it can be argued that your resume is most effective if it is customized to each job you apply for. Because every job has slightly different requirements, you might emphasize slightly different experiences or qualifications every time you apply for a position. If you have easy access to a word processor and are pretty good at using it—or you have a friend or colleague who can do the work for you at a reasonable cost—you might consider reshaping your resume every time you apply for a job. This also allows you to be sure that the right "keywords" are included in every resume. (See Chapter 14 for more information.)

Customizing your resume is not as difficult (or as wacky) as it might sound. When you know the requirements for a particular position you simply evaluate your resume, and the worksheets you used to prepare it, to see if you have presented yourself as a truly qualified candidate. Sometimes you will want to reorder your qualifications. Other times you may choose to expand the description of a particular experience that is especially relevant. The word processor allows you to move text around quickly, and the worksheets you completed earlier in this book give you the additional material you might want to use.

To print your customized resume, you can "output" directly from the word processor's printer onto nearly any paper you choose or you can go through any of the steps outlined above to produce a printed version. Obviously this approach makes the most sense when you have access to a printer that is able to produce a product you feel is ready to send. With this capability you can easily produce individualized resumes as well as individualized cover letters—and print both on the same paper as well.

If you are planning to look for work in more than one career field, you will probably need more than one version of your resume. It is common for job seekers to have a different version for each type of job they are seeking. Even if you choose not to customize your resume, you will want to have different resumes for different types of positions. For example, if you are planning to apply for jobs in sales and in marketing, you may want to consider having two resumes—one that empha-sizes your qualifications and experiences in sales and one that highlights your qualifications and experiences in marketing. You can have these photocopied or printed, and you can even have them put onto the same type of paper if you want to. Just remember which is which and use the resumes accordingly.

17 COVER LETTERS

BUILDING BRIDGES BETWEEN RESUMES AND JOBS

The cover letter is the letter that you will send to prospective employers along with your resume. It has a very clear purpose: the cover letter links your resume to the position you are seeking. It is a bridge that you construct between yourself and your employer-to-be. Whether you are applying for a specific job that is currently available or are simply asking what might be available, you will need a cover letter. In fact, your resume should never be put into the mail without a cover letter. Fortunately, a good cover letter is easy to prepare.

The key point to keep in mind when you write a cover letter is what you have to contribute to an employer. The most common mistake that job-seekers make in developing their cover letters is to focus on their own needs—the reasons that they are applying for positions. What employers want to know is what you can do for them—not what they can do for you. So, to write a successful cover letter, you have to think like an employer.

It might help you in writing your cover letters to picture yourself sitting at a desk opening one envelope after another, each one holding a resume and a cover letter. If you're like most employers, you will be making three piles out of these resumes and cover letters: YES (I think I'll call the person behind this resume and schedule an interview); MAYBE (the person I see described on paper looks kind of interesting, but not as interesting as the people in the YES pile); and NO (this candidate just doesn't look qualified). Your challenge is to get your cover letter and resume into the YES pile. A good cover letter can make the difference between the MAYBE pile and the YES pile. Since most employers never get beyond the YES stack, your cover letter has a vital part to play in your job search.

A COVER LETTER FOR EVERY RESUME

Not only do you have to send a cover letter with every resume you put into the mail, but you have to send a different letter with every resume. At the very least, you will change the address of your prospective employer and the title of the job you are applying for. When you are looking for only one kind of position, these small changes may be the only modifications you will need to make to your cover letter. However, if you are seeking different kinds of jobs, you will definitely need different types of cover letters.

This is not quite as intimidating as it sounds. As you will see below, cover letters are not very long and they are not very difficult to write. Avoid the temptation to say the same thing in every letter you write (and definitely avoid the temptation to have one letter printed or copied to accompany every resume you send). The extra time you spend on your cover letter can make the difference between getting called for an interview and being forgotten. If you are going to write, take the time to do it right.

WRITING THE COVER LETTER

There are only a few critical ingredients in a cover letter. Let's look at them in the order in which they will appear on paper.

Date

Write down the date and now you're on your way! (It's such a painless way to get started.)

Employer and address

Whenever possible, direct your letter and resume to a specific person, and include that person's title as well. If you don't know who the correct person is, pick up the telephone and call. If you don't do it now, you will kick yourself later when you want to follow up with another letter or call. Similarly, if you are not sure of the spelling of a name or the exact title of the person, call and find out. You will hurt your chances if you don't. (Nobody likes to have a name misspelled or a title misstated.) Obviously, you need to make sure that you have the address correct as well.

Salutation

If you know the gender of the person you are addressing, a simple "Dear Ms. _____" or "Dear Mr. _____" is fine. If you don't know the gender, call and ask (you won't be the only person who has ever inquired). If you really can't find out, write out the person's full name after the word "Dear." If you do not have a name in the address, simply skip the salutation altogether. (The days of writing "To whom it may concern" or "Dear sir or madam" are long gone.)

First paragraph: WHY

The first paragraph has one purpose: to state exactly WHY you are writing. Are you applying for a position that was advertised? If so, where was it advertised? Are you writing without knowing about an opening? If so, why did you pick this person or organization?

The first paragraph can be very brief, as you will see in the sample cover letters that follow.

Second paragraph: WHAT

In the second paragraph, you describe WHAT you have to offer to this particular employer. You can make general remarks about yourself, but try to back them up with specific examples if you can. This paragraph will probably change from one letter to another, although you may come up with phrases that you can use in more than one cover letter. For some letters, you might want to emphasize your experience, if it is directly relevant to a position you are seeking. In another, you may want to highlight your personal qualities, if they seem to match the requirements of the job. For still another letter, you could note your education, including individual courses you took that prepared you for the job you hope to secure. This is the spot where you build the "bridge" between your qualifications and the needs of the employer.

This paragraph is the heart of your cover letter. It shows the employer that you have thought about the job (or the organization) and believe that you can make a genuine contribution. (If you don't think that you can make a genuine contribution you probably shouldn't waste your time—and the employer's—by writing.) This is your chance to feature one or two specifics from your past that might positively impress a prospective employer. Have you taken on a project that demonstrates your initiative? Have you solved a problem in a way that saved time or money for a previous employer or organization? Have you faced challenges that are similar to those you are likely to face in this new position?

Feel free to "raid" your resume for examples and phrases. You can take any material in your resume and use it directly in your cover letter if it supports the point you want to make. You have already put a lot of effort into developing the wording of your resume and you do not have to reword it now if it works "as is." If it suits your purposes, use it. If not, rework it until it does. For example, you might want to add more detail about an accomplishment or a previous job in your cover letter than you included on your resume because the experience relates directly to the position you are applying for. One or two examples are all you need.

Remember: this is the place where you establish your qualifications. You want to "hook" the reader into reading your resume to find out more about you. Don't try to condense your whole resume into a one-paragraph summary. This part of the cover letter is just a "taste" of what is on the resume. Your challenge here is to make the reader want to find out more about you.

Third paragraph: HOW

This is your final paragraph. You want to let the reader know HOW to reach you to set up an interview. (Do you want to be called at work or at home? What are the best times to call?) You also want to state HOW you are going to proceed. (Are you going to call to follow up? If so, when?) Finally, you should state HOW you have responded to any specific requests the employer has made. (Were you asked to submit a sample of your previous work? A list of references?) Use this paragraph to address these requests.

Closing

Close your letter as you would any business letter. Use a businesslike closing word or phrase and follow it with your signature, your address, and your phone number(s). If you are using letterhead stationery that includes the address and phone number you want to use for contacts with prospective employers, you don't need to repeat the information in your closing.

You will find several different closing words on the sample cover letters that follow. Choose one that you like. Don't get too cute (don't use phrases like "Expectantly yours," for example). Remember that this is a business transaction and you will do fine.

A special note on "Salary History"

There is one request that is frequently made by employers in advertised openings that you DON'T have to address directly in your cover letters. This is the request for your "salary requirements" or for a "salary history." Unless you have very firm salary demands—so firm that you are willing to take yourself out of the running for a position even before you receive an interview—you should not name a precise dollar figure in your cover letter. Don't state exactly what you earn now and don't state what you expect your next job to pay.

Let's face it. There are many more factors to a job than salary alone. There may be a great benefits package to consider. Maybe the opportunities for advancement are tremendous. Or perhaps you're desperate for a job and would work for almost anything. Whatever your personal situation, the salary question is one that should be answered vaguely. It is perfectly acceptable to include a statement like "My salary requirements are flexible." You might follow that with "I will be happy to discuss them in an interview."

Even if you are sure that you know what the salary is when you are applying for a job, being vague in your cover letter can still pay off for you. Most jobs have salary ranges attached to them instead of one specific figure. You don't want to state an amount at the low end of the range because that is what you are likely to be offered if you get the job. At the same time, you don't want to give a figure at the high end of the range because you may be seen as greedy or out of the reach of the employer.

If you have a specific salary in mind, it is still best not to be too direct. For example, if you are making $34,000 per year now, you might say in your cover letter: "I expect that the position will offer a salary in the high 30's." Even if you know that the salary has a wide range, don't request a range yourself. (Don't write "I am looking for a job that pays in the mid to high 30's," because you are bound to be offered a salary at the low end of your own stated range.) Notice, too, in our example that the expectation was stated in terms of what the position might pay, not in terms of what the job seeker was demanding. Although employers believe that they want to hear the salary requirements of applicants, they often discriminate against candidates who directly state salary demands in their cover letters.

On the next page, you will find a checklist to use in evaluating your cover letter. Read it now, and then read it again after you have drafted a letter of your own. After the checklist there are several sample cover letters. None of these is exactly right for your situation, but you should be able to get direction and inspiration here for writing your own cover letters. Look these over and start writing.

COVER LETTER CHECKLIST

Use this checklist to critique your cover letters. If you can answer "yes" to every question, you have an excellent cover letter—and an excellent chance of getting an interview. If you can't answer "yes" to every question, go back and make a few changes to your letter.

1. Is your cover letter addressed to a specific person? (Are you sure that this is the correct person and that you have spelled the name and the title correctly?)

2. Does your letter state clearly why you are writing?

3. Does your letter tell the employer why you are qualified for the position you are seeking? Does it provide examples of your qualifications?

4. Does your letter tell an employer what you can contribute to the organization? Do you include accomplishments or personal qualifications that suggest the contributions you can make?

5. Does your letter highlight the most relevant facts about you and your background? Do you connect those facts directly to the needs of the employer?

6. Does your letter use "action words" to describe your accomplishments, skills, and qualifications?

7. Does your letter respond directly to an ad or job description? If so, does it address each of the points mentioned in the ad or description?

8. Does your letter avoid "jargon" that might not be understood by the recipient?

9. Is your letter persuasive? Does it encourage the reader to read the resume?

10. Does your letter avoid negative statements and apologies?

11. Have you cut out anything that seems vague or insincere?

12. Are the paragraphs short (no more than five lines each)?

13. Does your letter fit neatly onto one page?

14. Is your letter well typed and presented?

15. Does your letter include your name, address, and phone number?

January 10, 1998

Janet Schroeder, President
Schroeder Public Relations
119 Brattle Street
Cambridge, MA 02138

Dear Ms. Schroeder:

I am responding to your recent ad in the *Boston Globe*. I believe that I am well qualified for the position of Public Relations Associate and I know that I could make a significant contribution to your firm.

Although I have enclosed my resume, let me quickly highlight some of my relevant experiences. Through my in-depth internship at Morris-Bradshaw Public Relations, I had hands-on experience writing more than 25 press releases in less than four months. I followed through on all aspects of these releases, including their packaging and mailing. I have also written press releases for a local candidate for the Massachusetts state senate and conducted numerous phone surveys. I understand how a public relations firm works, I learn quickly, and I am comfortable working under deadlines.

I hope that we will be able to meet in person to discuss the Associate position. If I don't hear from you next week, I will give your secretary a call during the week of January 24th to see if I might make an appointment. I look forward to speaking with you soon.

Sincerely,

Helen Bueller

29 Oldbridge Road
Warwick, MA 01364

January 17, 1998

19 Westfield Avenue
Hartford, CT 06112

Ms. Joanne Ramirez, Principal
Oak Road Elementary School
1445 Oak Road Stratford, CT 06497

Dear Ms. Ramirez:

Nancy Brooks, a fourth grade teacher at Oak Road Elementary, has informed me that you have an opening for a second grade teacher for the school year that begins next September. I may be early in applying for the position but I believe I that I have a lot to offer to you and to your students.

I have enclosed my resume, which will present you with my background. What the resume cannot express is my enthusiasm for teaching children. Although I have only recently graduated from college, I have far more experience than most recent graduates. As you will see on my resume, I have taught third grade full-time, have substituted in every grade from kindergarten through sixth, and have volunteered as a Teacher's Aide for a year and a half. I am effective as a classroom teacher, tireless with children, and I can communicate well with fellow teachers and with parents.

I would like to have the opportunity to meet with you at your convenience. Although next fall seems like a long time from now, Nancy told me that you are hoping to fill the position by the end of February. I hope that I will hear from you by February 1. If I don't, I will give you a call to set up an appointment. I look forward to meeting you.

Sincerely,

Melinda Dalessio

January 24, 1998

James T. Chou
Software Applications Manager
Psy Tech, Inc.
11495 Lakeshore Drive
Minneapolis, MN 55429

Dear Mr. Chou:

I am writing to you because I believe that I could make a vital contribution to your division at Psy Tech. In my present position at Physical
Systems, Inc., I have developed software that meets the requirements
of physicists, hardware engineers, and systems programmers. I have
served as the primary systems representative in the physical sciences
lab. Since Psy Tech is in the same industry, I am sure that you have
similar needs in your division.

I have enclosed my resume, which will provide you with additional
information on my experience. You will see that I regularly troubleshoot
both hardware and software problems and train end users in software
applications.

I know that you may not have openings in your division at the present
time, but I think that it would be mutually beneficial for us to meet,
whether or not there are positions available. It is always worthwhile to
know more about the competition. Although our companies are not in
direct competition, I think it could pay to get together. I will give you a
call on February 1st to see when we can schedule an appointment.
Feel free to call me before then if it is more convenient for you. My
work number is (218) 972-1342.

Thank you in advance for your time and consideration.

Sincerely,

Orlando Titus

October 10, 1997

Hollis Horsten
Personnel Manager
Vacutron, Inc.
11929 Beach Road
Honolulu, Hl 96810

I am writing at the suggestion of Bruce Schwab, who works in your Quality Control Department. Bruce thinks that my skills in organizing and supervising would be an asset at Vacutron.

At present I am an Assistant Air Department Officer at the Naval Air Warfare Center in Honolulu. I expect to receive my honorable discharge from the Navy at the end of December. My experiences in the armed forces are directly relevant to your needs at Vacutron. As you will see on my resume, much of my military career has involved administration of large-scale operations. Currently I supervise 25 air traffic controllers, 15 equipment maintenance technicians, and 10 aircraft line handlers. In less than five years I have contributed to reducing the cost of aircraft maintenance by 25% and have overseen a reduction in staffing of 35%. I have personally supervised the transition of my department to a new computer system, running two systems in parallel for six months.

I think that these are exactly the kinds of skills that Vacutron could use. I would like the opportunity to discuss with you the ways in which I can make a contribution to the company. Please look over the resume that I have enclosed and give me a call. If I haven't heard from you by the end of next week, I will call you to set up an appointment. Even if you don't have a specific position in mind, or an immediate job opening, I think that our getting together will be worth your time. I look forward to speaking with you soon.

Sincerely,

Kent Zelinka

2903-B Kuaui Road
Honolulu, Hl 96816
(808) 982-2873

18 RESUME TIPS

WHAT TO DO AND WHAT NOT TO DO

DO!

1. "Hook" your readers. Near the top of your resume, include some key points about yourself that will make the reader want to find out more about you.

2. Highlight your strengths. You probably know the saying "If you've got it, flaunt it." This is certainly true on your resume. Your prospective employer should be able to see quickly what you have to offer.

3. Structure your resume like a pyramid. The most important things about you should be near the top. There is no formula that you have to follow in assembling the component parts of your resume, but you should start with your best features.

4. Be sure your resume is easy to read. If your resume is jammed with words, difficult to follow, or badly laid out on the page, no one is going to take the time to read it—even if you are a great job candidate.

5. Keep your sentences short. Start as many as you can with "action words" (a list of these is provided for you). It's OK to drop words like "a," "an," and "the."

6. Help your readers know what to read. Use boldface type. Use plenty of "white space" between points to make each point stand out.

7. Support your objective. If you have a job objective, be sure that your resume shows clearly why you are qualified for the job you are seeking.

8. Keep your resume to one or two pages. Most employers don't want to read more than two pages. They will read more if you are an incredibly experienced person with terrific credentials, but two-page resumes are safe.

9. If your resume is two pages, say so on page one. All you need to type is one line, like "Continued on next page."

10. Answer the question that every employer asks. Your resume must address the question that is in the employer's mind: "What can this person do for me?" If your resume can answer that question, you can get an interview—and an interview can land you a job.

DON'T!

1. Don't lie. You can never make a lie work in your favor. Don't stretch the truth too far either—it will break!

2. Don't copy someone else's resume. You can take inspiration from other resumes, including the samples in this book, and you can borrow elements from the resumes of others, but make your resume your own.

3. Don't write long sentences. Remember that your resume will be read quickly and set it up so that it can be read easily.

4. Don't use long lines. Lines that run all the way across a page take too long to read and make it easy for readers to lose interest.

5. Don't put more than four lines together in one "block." If you have more than four short lines, you are probably trying to say too much. Divide a long block of text into two points.

6. Don't be vague. Be as specific as possible. Include facts and figures wherever you can.

7. Don't include information that is not relevant to an employer. There is a good rule to follow in evaluating whether or not something is relevant: "If in doubt, leave it out."

8. Don't include "personal" information. There is almost never a need to include such data as your height, weight, age, marital status, number of children, etc. This kind of information hasn't been included in resumes for more than twenty years and most employers would be shocked and dismayed to see it.

9. Don't list a reference unless you have the person's permission. Of course, it's important too to know that you will get a positive recommendation!

10. Don't build your resume around dates. Dates should be put at the end of any description—not at the beginning—or they should be left out altogether.

19 SAMPLE RESUMES

On the following pages you will find more than eighty sample resumes. All are based on the resumes of real people. (However, their names, addresses, phone numbers, names of employers, and dates have been changed.) There are many ways to use these sample resumes to improve your own resume. Here are some suggestions on what to look for when you study the resumes that follow:

1) **Organization**. Examine how each resume is organized. Take a look at the overall structure. Remember that key "selling points" should be near the top of each resume, just as your selling points should be at the top of yours.

2) **Phrasing**. Although you won't find a whole resume here that you can use as your own, you may find specific phrases that can help you express a skill or accomplishment or personal qualification.

3) **Design**. There is no single "look" that a resume must have. There are a number of resume designs in these samples. One of them may reach out and grab you, or you might want to incorporate several different component parts when you design your own.

4) **Occupations**. It's a myth that all resumes in a certain occupation look alike and use the same phrasing. However, you might want to examine how other people in your field have presented themselves in their resumes. But don't restrict yourself to just one occupation. Look at several before you decide how you want to present yourself in your own.

5) **Problems**. Many of the people whose resumes appear here had to solve problems, perhaps the same problems you face as you put together your own resume. Look through these samples to see their solutions. Check the notes at the bottom of each resume, since these comments often point out problems and solutions.

Take your time as you browse through the sample resumes. You can learn a lot from them!

"BEFORE" RESUME

Melinda Dalessio
19 Westfield Ave.
Hartford, CT 06112
(203) 846-2291

Career Objective
To obtain a teaching position at the elementary level.

Education
University of Hartford, Hartford, CT
Graduate-Level Teacher Certification Program, Pre-K through grade 8
Graduation and Certification, May 1995

University of Massachusetts, Boston
B.A. English 1991

Professional Experience

Hartford School District, Hartford, CT
March, 1995-May, 1995, Jefferson Elementary School, Hartford, CT
Student Teacher Internship
* 14 weeks full-time teaching 3rd Grade

January, 1994-February, 1995, Hartford School District Certified Substitute K-6
* Substituted K-6 all levels

Sept. 1993-January, 1995, Jefferson Elementary School Classroom Volunteer
* Volunteered in both kindergarten and 6th grade classrooms

Work Experience
August, 1991-August 1992, Carousel Fashions, Boston, Mass.
* Assistant Manager

1987-present, seasonal, Dalessio Travel, Bristol, CT
* Administrative Assistant

Sept. 1992-August 1993, Limited Express, Hartford, CT
* Sales Associate

Note: This resume doesn't tell an employer very much about what Melinda has to offer. It is simply a chronicle of what she has done in the past.

"AFTER" RESUME

MELINDA DALESSIO
19 Westfield Ave
Hartford, CT 06112
(203) 846-2291

CAREER OBJECTIVE
To obtain a teaching position at the elementary level.

SKILLS
- Teaching children reading, writing, and thinking in a variety of subjects
- Managing time effectively
- Maintaining order and helping children resolve interpersonal conflicts
- Giving clear directions

PERSONAL QUALIFICATIONS
- Patient
- Able to work cooperatively as part of a larger unit
- Good with children and parents
- Able to pay attention to several tasks simultaneously

PROFESSIONAL EXPERIENCE

Student Teacher Internship - Jefferson Elementary School, Hartford, Connecticut
(March 1995 - May 1995)
- 14 week full-time position teaching 3rd Grade

Certified Hartford School District Substitute Teacher K-6
- Substituted K-6 levels (January 1994 - February 1995)

Classroom Volunteer, Jefferson Elementary School
(September 1993 - January 1995)
- Volunteered in both Kindergarten and 6th grade classrooms

EDUCATION
University of Hartford, Hartford, CT
Graduate-Level Teacher Certification Program,
Pre-K through Grade 8 with a focus on Whole Language
Graduation and Certification, May 1995

University of Massachusetts, Boston, MA   B.A., English 1991

My complete credentials are on file in the Office of Educational Placement at
the University of Hartford. They can be forwarded at your request.

---

*Note: Here Melinda "comes alive." She speaks directly to the needs of an employer
and stresses what she has to offer.*

"BEFORE" RESUME

Helen Bueller • 29 Oldbridge Road • Warwick, MA 01364 • (617) 973-3662

EDUCATION:

B.A. University of Massachusetts, Boston 1995
Major: Speech and Communication

EMPLOYMENT:

Community Head Start, Warwick, MA
Assistant Teacher, Summer 1993

Central States Sports Schools, Warwick, MA
Softball instructor in girls' sports camp, Summer 1992

INTERNSHIP:

Morris-Bradshaw Public Relations, Boston, MA
Student Intern in public relations firm, Summer 1994

VOLUNTEER EXPERIENCE:

Citizens for Christine Powers, Boston, MA
Student volunteer in campaign of state senate candidate,
October 1992

COLLEGE EXPERIENCE:

University of Massachusetts, Boston, MA
Tour guide leader, 1992 - 93, 1993 - 94, 1994 - 95
Student Activities Council
Vice-President, 1994 - 95
Membership Committee, 1993 - 94

Note: In this "Before" resume, Helen overemphasizes positions and dates. She tells very little about her qualifications or accomplishments. She looks like thousands of other recent graduates.

Vernon Quennell
140 Iroquois Avenue Kokomo, IN 46901 (317) 987-1450

OBJECTIVE:
>   A position as administrative assistant or executive secretary

QUALIFYING SKILLS:
- Experienced in a variety of office settings.
- Proficient in the use of numerous software packages, including WordPerfect, Xywrite, and Word for Windows.
- Able to complete complex assignments on tight deadlines.
- Skilled in interpersonal relations, on the telephone and face-to-face.
- Extensive knowledge of travel planning.
- Competent in bookkeeping and basic accounting.

EXPERIENCE:
>   Assistant to the President
>   Oribtron Industries
>   Assistant to Director of Marketing
>   Chromalux, Inc.
>   Executive Secretary
>   Betacom Communications
>   Executive Assistant
>   Woodruff Transportation
>   All positions were of short duration, obtained through Action Temporary Service, Kokomo, IN (7/94 - Present)
>
>   Travel Counselor, Diners Club Travel Related Services, Bowie MD (10/91 - 12/93)
>   Responsible for travel arrangements for Diners Club members worldwide.

EDUCATION:
>   Lake Forest College, Lake Forest, IL
>   Major: Business and Communications
>   Attended: 1989 - 1991
>
>   College of Travel and Tourism, Cocoa, FL
>   Diploma, August 1991

Note: In this resume, Vernon highlights his skills and experience in office positions. His other resume is focused on travel.

KARL BOYTON

4 Plower Drive
Somerville, MA 02145
(508) 892-2312 Office
(508) 892-4213 Ans. Service

CAREER SUMMARY

Over 15 years experience maintaining and repairing Air Conditioning, Refrigeration and Commercial Electrical Products. My experience, combined with knowledge gained from running my own business, can contribute to any maintenance program or organization.

EMPLOYMENT HISTORY

Owner/Operator, BOYTON SERVICE COMPANY, Somerville, MA   (10/91-Present)

Responsible for the day to day operations of a successful commercial and residential air conditioning, heating and electrical repair and installation company.

• Manage three employees
• Ensure company profitability
• Oversee sub-contractors (up to 15 per year)
• Purchase, install and repair commercial kitchens for hospitals and restaurants
• Repair and sell used electrical equipment with quality service

Manager, Maintenance and Repairs, FRIENDLY'S ICE CREAM PARLORS   (10/88-10/91)

Sole individual responsible for maintaining refrigeration, air-conditioning, electrical equipment, plumbing and heating for 10 Friendly's franchises throughout region.

• Hired sub-contractors
• Purchased equipment and parts amounting to $40,000 to $50,000 per year
• Oversaw sub-contractors during the building of new locations and repair of existing locations

HVAC "A" Mechanic, DIGITAL EQUIPMENT CORPORATION   (2/86-10/88)

Responsibilities involved the maintenance and repair of various chillers, compressors, motor control stations, hot water and steam heating systems, exhaust hoods for laboratory use, cooling water towers, pumping systems (electric and steam turbine).

• Maintained and repaired 10 Edpack computer room coolers and 19 microprocessor controlled constant temperature chambers

SEE NEXT PAGE

KARL BOYTON EMPLOYMENT HISTORY (continued)

- Diagnosed electronic, electric and pneumatic control systems, air balance and calibration of VAV equipment, Powers 600 computer system and boiler maintenance
- Supervised up to six workers when required

HVAC Mechanic, BOSTON MEDICAL CENTER   (4/84-2/86)

Responsibilities included the maintenance, repair and installation of various chillers, pneumatic equipment and controls, air compressors, vacuum pumps, commercial refrigeration, heating systems, water tower, water pumps and a domestic hot water system

- Performed arc and gas welding, brazing, blueprint reading and pipefitting
- Troubleshot wiring problems and various related maintenance jobs

HVAC Installer, YANKEE MANUFACTURING COMPANY   (8/83-4/84)

Responsibilities included installation of heaters (gas and oil), air cleaners, air conditioners, full conversions, duct-work, and thermostats.

- Made custom duct-work
- Bought various equipment for installation
- Performed all aspects of sheet metal fabrication

EDUCATION

MASSACHUSETTS TECHNICAL INSTITUTE, Boston, MA
September 1983-January 1984
Air Conditioning and Refrigeration

CAMBRIDGE COMMUNITY COLLEGE, Boston, MA
January 1984-Present
Air Conditioning and Refrigeration (Electrical Controls, Electronics)

SPECIAL COURSES/SEMINARS ATTENDED

Bitzer Steam Heating Seminar; Trane Centrifugal Seminar;
Chemtrol PVC Pipefitting Seminar; Black Seal Preparation Course;
Betz Chemicals Steam Boiler Seminar; Welding Course;
Honeywell Pneumatic Control Set-up and Maintenance Seminar

AWARDS

Certificate of Merit, Massachusetts Technical Institute, January 1984

Note: Karl promotes his experience by presenting his responsibilities and then highlighting key features. His resume demands a second page.

SAMUEL LACROIX
144 Wiggins Ave., Apt. 2
Elkhart, IN 46516

(317) 769-8223 (car)
(317) 742-4689 (home)

QUALIFICATIONS

Sales professional, with accomplishments in sales and sales management in commercial accounts and retail establishments selling varied products.

Experienced in all phases of the sales process - - prospecting, closing sales, customer and credit follow-up.

• Able to quickly apply sales experience to new products.

• A "self-starter" and tireless worker who produces results.

EXPERIENCE

Area Manager, Commercial Division, Alta Fuels Co., Elkhart, IN (1992 to present)

Total responsibility for developing a new commercial division of independent fuel company. Responsibilities included generating prospects, selling, credit and customer service of newly originated commercial accounts.

• Established new commercial sales division

• Increased sales from zero gallons to 2.5 million gallons in six months

Area Manager, Enviro, Inc., Kokomo, IN   (1987-1992)
Responsible for geographic area within commercial division of fuel company. Respon sibilities included prospecting, placing orders, credit and customer serviceof commercial accounts.

• Built business unit from zero gallons to 6 million gallons in sales of fuel products to large commercial accounts such as UPS, Upland Dairy, and others

• Developed new sales regions in Kokomo and Elkhart

• Called on all levels of management, including VP's, General Managers, Purchasing Managers, and others

CONTINUED ON NEXT PAGE

SAMUEL LACROIX
Page 2

Sales Representative, A-I Chemical Products, Gary, IN　　　　　(1985-1987)

Responsible for calling on new and existing accounts to place janitorial cleaning supplies, chemicals and paper products. Handled all phases of sales process.

• Exceeded sales goals on a regular basis

• Signed up more than 50 new accounts in 3 years

Route Driver/Sales Representative, Uniform Cleaning Services, Grand Rapids, MI
(1982-1985)

Responsible for calling on new and existing accounts to secure uniform cleaning services

• Received performance bonus each year.

• Added more than 10 new, large-volume customers each year

Retail Store Manager, Kinney Shoes, Grand Rapids, MI　　　　　(1983-1985)

Total responsibility for all operations of retail shoe store.Responsibilities included all personnel functions, training, merchandising,budgets and expenses.

• Managed from 8 - 12 employees in several different stores

• Increased annual sales to more than $3 million in each store

PERSONAL
• Can speak conversational French and some Italian

• Volunteer fundraiser for Muscular Dystrophy Foundation for more than 10 years. Have personally raised over $1 million.

• Volunteer assistant in pediatric physical therapy department of St. Xavier Hospital, Elkhart, TN

Note: Salespeople need to demonstrate their sales accomplishments. Sam does this job by job. He never attended college, so he doesn't have a section for education. He uses the "Personal " heading to show that he has a life beyond work.

ALBERT INGALLS
117 1/2 Chestnut Street
Flint, MI 48506
(313) 882-1976

OCCUPATIONAL OBJECTIVE

Experienced journeyman Pipefitter/Plumber seeks position where varied skills can be applied.

EXPERIENCE SUMMARY

Inspect, repair, adjust, install and maintain all piping and associated equipment in a major production plant. Ability to trouble-shoot and repair problems with hydraulic and pneumatic production machinery. Experience with high pressure steam, air, gas, water, acids, chemicals and sewer and waste treatment procedures.

Working experience on steel butt-weld pipe, stainless steel, cast iron, saran, P.V.C., copper, black iron screwed and sprinkler systems for fire control. Maintenance and repair of all plumbing systems, steam heating and hot water heat both industrially and commercially.

Practical knowledge of all power tools, pipe threading machines, hand tools, measuring devices, burning and soldering equipment associated with the pipefitting and plumbing trade.Expertise in the removal of asbestos on piping and other areas (hold Michigan State permit).

EMPLOYMENT HISTORY

Pipefitter/Hydraulic
Fisher Guide Division of General Motors, Flint, MI (1/90 - present)

Residential Plumber
Plumber's and Pipefitters Union #12, Escanaba, MI (2/88-1/90)

Journeyman Pipefitter/Plumber
USX Corporation, Flint, MI (9/86-2/88)

Residential Plumber, Ace Home Heating, Detroit, MI (4/83-9/86)

EDUCATIONAL BACKGROUND

Apprenticeship, Pipefitter/Plumber - USX Corporation
Four-year program - Journeyman, Certification

HVAC Certification Program - Metropolitan Community College

Note: Al clearly describes his skills in the "Experience Summary" and straightforwardly shows how and where he acquired those skills.

CAROL LANSDOWNE   316-932-1 749 (Office)
19 Cedar Crest   316-897-1 455 (Pager)
Wichita, KS 67205   316-382-2365 (Home)

SUMMARY

Experienced attorney, member of the Bar in Kansas and Texas, with extensive work in litigation: discovery, depositions, motions, proof hearings, trials, and legal research. Skilled in matrimonial and family law, as well as commercial litigation.

EDUCATION

University of Texas at Austin   Baylor University
J.D., 1983, with distinction   B.S., Psychology, 1980
Honors: Law Review,   Honors: Phi Beta Kappa
Moot Court Competition

EXPERIENCE

Associate, Kramer and Heldref, Wichita, KS (1992- present)

- Staff attorney in general law practice. Responsible for all aspects of practice.
- Trial experience in Municipal Court, Superior Court, Federal Court, and Common Pleas Court.
- Specialize in commercial litigation, often involving extensive research. Involved in actions worth more than $20 million since joining firm.

Staff Attorney, Holden and Calder, Dallas, Texas (1987-1992)

- High-volume, metropolitan law firm, with broad general practice.
- Litigation involved personal injury and commercial cases.
- Handled wide range of legal activities, from real estate to wills and trusts.

Staff Attorney, Legal Aid Society, Fort Worth, TX (1985-1987)

- Provided legal representation to all clients who met low-income guidelines.
- Extensive courtroom experience.
- Legal work in child custody, criminal law, motor vehicle, and many other areas.

PERSONAL
- Volunteer Attorney, Legal Aid Society of Wichita
- Near fluency in spoken Spanish

Note: Carol emphasizes her experience. She lists her education first because it is so impressive. Notice her clear summary of her experience.

BARRY EVERETT • 112 Folkstone Ave. • Decatur, GA 30035 • (404) 642-7319

CAREER SUMMARY
Over ten years progressive credit analysis and collection experience dealing with commercial, individual and government accounts with demonstrated accomplishments.

EXPERIENCE
Major Accounts Analyst
GENERAL MANUFACTURING, INC., Atlanta, GA
Total responsibility for the credit maintenance and collection of 40 + major accounts of minimum $1,000,000 net sales, including addressing problems, keeping invoices in good condition and ensuring that accounts stay within credit limits.
* Reduced over-90-day receivables by more than 50%
* Lowered account maintenance paper work by 70%
* Improved "skipped invoice" process, increasing receivables
* Maintained rapport with sales force achieving satisfactory problem resolutions

Credit and Collections Administrator
GATEWAY, INC., Augusta, GA
Total responsibility for credit and collections for entire accounts receivable, including making credit decisions, commission due reports and journal entries for write-offs and adjustments.
* Implemented use of Dun & Bradstreet and NACM credit decision process
* Reduced over-90-day receivables by more than 20%
* Utilized negotiation and communication skills to develop payment schedules and improve long-term business relationships with problem accounts

Junior Accountant/Credit & Collection
COMPUTER ASSOCIATES, Tucker, GA
Primary functions involved handling credit and collection of private sector, military and government software lease, lease/purchase and maintenance contracts.
* Conducted contract reviews assuring that commitments were within authorized limits
* Communicated with sales force to evaluate and resolve problem accounts

EDUCATION
DeKalb County College, Decatur, GA
Associates Degree in Applied Science with Major in Business

SKILLS
Working knowledge of IBM PC/Compatible hardware and software;
VAX 11-780; Altos Computer; WordPerfect 5.1; E-Mail

Note: Barry has not been continuously employed, so he avoids dates altogether. This puts the focus on what he has done and not when he did it.

BENNO LIKUNEN

1779 Maple Drive, Oak Park, IL 60302
(312) 797-3535 Office
(312) 688-2315 Pager

SUMMARY Experienced plant manager with recognized expertise in management of medical centers. Effective supervisor with a commitment to excellence.

EXPERIENCE

Director of Plant Operations, St. Thomas Medical Center, Oak Park, IL (1987-1995)

Responsibilities and Accomplishments

- Responsible for $6 million annual budget
- Supervise 35 maintenance, power plant and biomedical engineering personnel, through an Assistant Director of Plant Operations and four supervisors.
- Established an in-house biomedical engineering department, realizing over $40,000 in yearly savings
- Obtained a federal grant to partially finance a new Energy Management System, resulting in savings of approximately $150,000 per year
- Installed a new incinerator with heat recovery, saving the hospital over $1 million per year
- Initiated, organized and coordinated a 12-week training program for all new maintenance personnel
- Acted as the owner's representative in all phases of construction of a $45 million addition, bringing the construction to completion on schedule

Note: Medical Center merged with St. Peter's Hospital January 1, 1996

Director of Engineering and Maintenance, Dekalb Community Hospital (1982-1987)
Maintenance Supervisor, Cook County Hospital (1979-1982)
Director of Engineering, Quincey Rehabilitation Center (1975-1979)

EDUCATION

Graduate of Cook County Vocational Technical School
Major: Power Plant Engineering

Maintained continuing education through numerous seminars on all phases of engineering, management, design and construction, and codes and standards given by the Joint Commission on Accreditation of Healthcare Organizations, the American Society for Hospital Engineering, and other state, federal and private educational agencies.

PROFESSIONAL SOCIETIES & AFFILIATIONS

President & Trustee, Executive Hospital Engineers of Illinois
Trustee, National Power Engineers
Vice Chairman, Engineering Advisory Board of Illinois Hospital Association
Member, American Society for Hospital Engineering
Member, National Fire Protection Association

Note: Benno emphasizes his most recent job and then implies the reason it has ended.

BRANDON K. TRAMORE
415 Hollister Road
Pocatello, Idaho 83204 (208) 394-1779

CAREER SUMMARY
Over 25 years of Law Enforcement experience, attaining expert status in the areas of Domestic Violence, Crime Scene Investigation, and use of Breathalyzer.

EXPERIENCE

POCATELLO POLICE DEPARTMENT (December 1970 - Present)
Sergeant (June 1993 - Present)
* Supervised up to 48 Patrol Officers within all areas of the department
* Supervised and trained officers in Domestic Violence investigation and arrest
* Functioned as leading Crime Scene Investigator for the department
* Worked closely with State Police and County Prosecutor in the solving of crimes

Detective Patrol Officer (May 1990 - May 1993)
* Handled criminal investigations and preparation of cases for court
* Gathered facts by conducting interviews, collected evidence and observed activities of suspects for criminal cases
* Performed fingerprint classification, latent fingerprint identification and firearm identification at the crime scene

Patrol Officer (December 1970 - May 1990)
* Performed regular patrol duties during rapid growth period of the department

TRAINING AND EDUCATION
* Law Enforcement Officers Training School, conducted by the FBI, 1995
* Idaho State Police, Department of Public Safety, Breathalyzer Course, 1995
* Western States Police Institute, Police Management Course, November 1993
* Police Training Institute, "Kinesic Interview and Interrogation" Seminar, 1992
* Idaho State Police Technical Bureau, six week, 240 hour course in Forensic Sciences, including Fingerprint Classification, Latent Fingerprint Identification, and Criminalistics at the Special and Technical Services Section, May, 1991
* Idaho State Police, Drug Enforcement Course, 1982
* Six week resident Basic Training Police Course - Boise, Idaho, 1970

ASSOCIATIONS
Member: International, National and Idaho Identification Association
Member: Idaho Detectives Association

Note: Brandon has only worked for one employer. He details clearly his experience and training.

CLARENCE L. INNIS
212 Holloway Ave.
Baton Rouge, LA 70816
(504) 788-3675

EMPLOYMENT OBJECTIVE
A Fleet Maintenance Mechanic/Auto Body Repair position that will utilize my professional skills.

PROFESSIONAL EXPERIENCE
Automotive   Mechanic
Duties
- Repairs, overhauls and maintains foreign and domestic automobiles, vans and trucks.
- Discusses the description of the problem with the customer or reads work order
- Examines or test drives vehicle to determine nature and extent of repairs or services
- Quickly and efficiently prepares written estimates
- Applies knowledge of automotive electronics and mechanics to diagnose problems
- Employs expertise of auto body to repair damaged vehicles efficiently and effectively

Skills and Knowledge
- Meets all LA automotive mechanic and auto body repair certification requirements
- Working experience with on-board diagnostic computers
- Removes units such as engine, transmission, truck transfer case or differential
- Uses hoist, hand tools, micrometers, gauges, wrenches, machine tools and front-end alignment equipment
- Repairs and overhauls standard automotive systems such as cooling, air-conditioning, electrical, fuel, exhaust, brake, advanced electronics, front-end and steering systems

EMPLOYMENT HISTORY
1991 - Present   Automotive Technician
                        Avery Ford, Baton Rouge, LA

1990 - 1991   Automotive Mechanic and Body Repairman
                        Sam's Auto Body Service, Baton Rouge, LA

1988 - 1990   Automotive Mechanic and Body Repairman
                        C&J Auto Body, Laplace, LA

EDUCATION and TRAINING
Computer Diagnostics, Ford Motor Co.
ASE Certified Air Conditioning Technician
Laplace High School, Laplace, LA, Graduated 1988

Note: Clarence does a nice job of articulating his duties and skills. The emphasis on dates is intentional, to show that he has been steadily employed.

CLAUDIA TU

17 Prairie Ct.
Helena, MT 59601
(406) 762-3219

SUMMARY

Over 15 years of service to the citizens of Montana, progressing fromClerk-Stenographer to Administrative Secretary. Have received consecutive outstanding evaluations, based on efficient and effective performance, attention to detail, and high level of professionalism.

EXPERIENCE

Administrative Secretary,
Division of Environmental Protection
State of Montana

- Report directly to the assistant administrator of the Office of Statewide Operations
- Provide all secretarial services to the assistant administrator
- Collect and assemble information required for management reports and meetings
- Maintain appointment calendar
- Organize meetings as directed
- Prepare correspondence for signature of supervisor
- Monitor payroll time reports with office
- Communicate regularly with key personnel in other state offices

Previous positions with the State of Montana include Clerk-Stenographer, Senior Clerk-Stenographer, and Principal Clerk-Stenographer. Career began as Clerk-Typist in private industry.

SKILLS AND ACCOMPLISHMENTS

- Proficient in use of Microsoft Word on Macintosh computers
- Organized statewide three-day meeting on the topic of "Clean Water 2000." More than 75 people attended.
- Served as co-chairperson for United Way campaign in the Division of Environmental Protection. Raised over $200,000, a 5% increase over previous year.

EDUCATION

- Enrolled in Associate of Applied Science degree program in Business, Community College of Helena
- Have participated in 12 professional seminars offered by the State Department of Personnel during the last 10 years.

Note: Claudia thought she was, in her words, "just a secretary," until she completed the worksheets that led her to this resume!

DANIELLE KING
8 Brockton Road
Bar Harbor, ME 04609
(207) 699-3821

CAREER OBJECTIVE: Restaurant Management

WORK EXPERIENCE:
The Laughing Mermaid, Bar Harbor, ME
High-volume restaurant and night club in affluent tourist area.

General Manager
- Supervised all aspects of operation of 200-seat dining room, nightclub, kitchen and banquet facilities, including budgets, personnel, purchasing and cost control.
- Created and implemented staff training programs in all positions which resulted in consistent increase in business during my tenure through improved service.
- Coordinated various employee functions to maintain high morale and encourage group cohesiveness, which played a major role in continuous reduction of turnover. 11/93 - Present

Operations Manager
- Directed operation of high volume night-club (capacity 300), including inventory management, personnel, purchasing and staff scheduling.
- Designed and executed all facets of marketing plan, including newspaper, radio and in-house advertising.

EDUCATION:
B.A., Economics/PublicAdministration, 1992
University of Maine, Orono
- Member of the National Honor Society in Economics (Omicron Delta Epsilon)
- Member of the National Honor Society in Spanish Language (Alpha Mu Gamma)
- Dean's List - Fall 1992, Fall 1993

VOLUNTEER WORK:
Founder and organizer of annual Bar Harbor dinner dance for American Cancer Society since 1993

REFERENCES: Available upon request.

- Fluent in Spanish
- Willing to relocate nationally or internationally

Note: Danielle compresses a large number of responsibilities into a compact presentation of experience. This resume will not "scan" well, but probably will not be scanned.

DEBORAH HACKING
719 Flamingo Way
Naples, FL 33942
(305) 975-1637

CAREER SUMMARY
More than 15 years of progressively responsible experience in retail banking, including:
- Start-up of new branch bank
- Supervision of all aspects of branch
- Development of extensive loan portfolios

EXPERIENCE
Assistant Vice President - Manager and Commercial Loan Officer
FLORIDA NATIONAL BANK, Naples, FL
- Managed $13.5 million branch from its inception
- Supervised staff of 9 employees
- Utilized cold calls, telemarketing and referrals to develop $11 million in commercial loans and $3 million in demand deposits
- Exceeded goals for business development, total branch deposit growth and expense control

Retail Banking Officer- Branch Manager
COMMUNITY BANK OF FLORIDA, Naples, FL
- Managed the largest branch office in the district with deposits of $17 million and a staff of 10 people
- Met mandate to develop community involvement and new business development

Assistant Vice President - Manager of Office and Loan Officer
THE BANK OF DELRAY, Delray Beach, FL
- Managed the 5th largest office in the system with deposits approaching $36 million and a staff of 15 people
- Established new commercial business through an officer calling program
- Administered a loan portfolio of approximately $2 million

Regional Loan Representative
SARASOTA NATIONAL BANK, Sarasota, FL
- Administered loan portfolio of approximately 50 loans totaling $7 million
- Analyzed financial statements, prepared loan presentation and initial credit decision recommendation and maintained credit files

EDUCATION
Bachelor of Science, Business; Concentrations in Accounting and Management
FLORIDA STATE UNIVERSITY, Tallahassee, Florida

Note: Deborah held some of these positions for a very short time. However, by dropping dates and emphasizing her accomplishments, she has created a fine resume.

Emily F. Roy
240 Gallivan Boulevard
Dorchester, MA 02124
(617) 872-3439

CAREER OBJECTIVE: A position in Corporate Accounting

HIGHLIGHTS:
- ✓ Earned 3 promotions in less than 5 years.
- ✓ Due to excellent performance, promoted to 3 positions that require a Bachelor's degree.
- ✓ Received Quality Award for work performed in organizing Corporate Quality Conference.
- ✓ Invited to join inter-company Accounting Procedures Quality Action Team that formulated procedures for post-merger transfers between business units.
- ✓ Taught computer packages such as Lotus, Easytrieve and Displaywrite to subordinates.
- ✓ Computerized daily worksheets and reconciliations previously perfomed manually.
- ✓ Computer experience includes: Lotus, DOS, Easytrieve, TSO, MSA, MacCormick & Dodge, Telegraf and Harvard Graphics

EXPERIENCE:
Data General, Boston, MA
 Accounts Payable Supervisor 11/93 - Present
- ✓ Supervised revitalization/reorganization of Accounts Payable Department.
- ✓ Implemented new procedures and controls.
- ✓ Retrain personnel for more efficient and productive operations.

John Hancock, Inc., Boston, MA
 Trust Accounting Department Accounting Clerk (Temporary) 9/93 - 11/93

Massachusetts Transportation Authority, Boston, MA
 Accounts Payable Department Processor (Temporary) 6/92 - 9/93

Chemtel Corp., Weston, MA
 Corporate Accounts Payable Supervisor 10/87 - 6/92
- ✓ Supervised staff of 15-19 in processing payment of 161,000 invoices plus 72,000 expense reports for a total of $890 million annually.
- ✓ Developed and implemented corporate policies and procedures; oversaw system enhancements.

EDUCATION:
 Babson College, Babson Park, MA
 Anticipate receiving B.S. degree in Accounting, June 1996.
 Community College of Boston
 A.A.S., Accounting, 1987

Note: Emily successfully integrates temporary work into her "experience." She has an especially nice mixture of highlights. If Emily submits her resume electronically, she will want to remove the checkmarks.

EVE ELIAS

128 Riverfront Drive
Apartment B-6
Independence, MO 64050

(417) 599-2811 Office
(417) 599-1712 Home

OBJECTIVE

Experienced staff accountant (C.P.A.) seeks position leading to partner status.

EXPERIENCE

Accountant, Anderson-Little, Independence, MO (7/92- present)
- Responsible for compilations, reviews and audits for various clients. Prepare financial statements, management letters, tax returns and payroll forms.
- Conduct all phases of an audit reporting directly to partner. Responsibilities include supervisory duties and administrative functions.
- Analyze brokerage portfolios through summarization of investment activity to determine return on investment.
- Represent the firm at college recruitment meetings with graduating seniors.

Accounting Intern, Guttman and Gonzales, Columbia, MO (Summer 1991)
- Member of the project team responsible for the development of a uniform chart of accounts.
- Used general ledger systems to research and summarize general ledger account activity by journal entry type.
- Assisted in the summarizing of production credit information for institutional sales offices performing directed business.
- Prepared and updated Lotus spreadsheets for analysis of profit and loss statements.

CERTIFICATIONS

Certified Public Accountant

EDUCATION

University of Missouri, Columbia, MO
Degree: Bachelor of Science, June 1992
Major: Accounting

GPA: 3.2
Honors: Dean's List
Trustees Scholarship.

SKILLS

LOTUS 1-2-3, ATB, T-Value and Financial Reporting

Note: Eve provides a good example of how to present a summer internship as if it were a full-time job.

Jonathan Dietrich
1930-A Clyde Court
Norfolk, VA 23513
(804) 793-3211

OVERVIEW

Aircraft Mechanic seeking position where the experience, education and training I have gained in the military can be effectively applied in the commercial airline industry

EDUCATION

- Completed PAA Flight Safety Course
- PAA License in A & P Mechanics
  Aviation Test Center, Tullahoma, TN
- Completed Primary Leadership Development Course
  US Army, Fort Rucker, AL

ACCOMPLISHMENTS

- Overhauled 21 aircraft over 2 year time-frame
- Finished maintenance at least 1 week prior to scheduled delivery date
- Conducted 300 hour annual overhauls
- Functioned as Phase Team Leader
- Learned FAA flight safety rules and regulations as Non-Commissioned Officer in charge of the Aerial Recovery Team
- Supervised 5 helicopter Crew Chiefs and 6 aircraft

EMPLOYMENT

US Army:
- Aircraft Mechanic, Saudi Arabia, Iraq, Kuwait
  Operations Desert Shield & Storm
- Line Chief, Helicopter Repair, Fort Hood, TX
- Aircraft Mechanic, APO NY

AWARDS

- Silver Star
- Bronze Star with Valor
- 2 Legions of Merit
- The National Defense Service Medal

Note: No dates are included here because Jon's "career" is very brief. The emphasis is on his accomplishments.

FRANCINE HANCOCK
934 Highland Street
Valdosta, GA 31602
(912) 874-931 2

CAREER OBJECTIVE: Seeking a position in Banking, Credit, or Customer Service.

STRENGTHS: Over ten years of experience in finance and banking-related fields.

EXPERIENCE:

<u>Cashier</u>, Valdosta State College, Valdosta, GA 1/94-present
* Cash personal checks, credit union checks, process petty cash vouchers and expense reports
* Organize and distribute bi-monthly payrolls
* Order and maintain cash balance
* Sell travelers checks, accept payments for miscellaneous accounts and refunds to company
* Summarize and account for all financial activity

<u>Head Teller/Assistant Operations Manager</u>
First National Bank of Georgia, Valdosta, GA 10/91-1/94
* Supervise and evaluate bank tellers
* Order and ship cash; maintain cash level in branch
* Oversee audits and safe deposits
* Buy and sell foreign currency; prepare international drafts
* Extensive customer service; MAC machine settlement

<u>Senior Client Services Representative</u>
Lowndes County Medical Center, Valdosta, GA 10/88-10/91
* Oversee financial services for patients and staff
* Telephone and written correspondence with physicians and other medical providers
* Monthly summary and analysis of Credit Union activities
* Assist internal as well as external auditors
* Special accounting projects as assigned by manager

<u>Teller and Platform Assistant</u>, First Bank of Lowndes, Valdosta, Ga 1/87-10/88
* Teller functions
* Open savings and checking accounts
* Interview potential loan candidates

EDUCATION:
B.S., Business Administration
Valdosta State College, Anticipated 1996

REFERENCES: Available upon request

Note: Francine is an adult learner presently enrolled in college. Although she has not had high-level jobs, she articulates her responsibilities well. For electronic scanning, Francine will need to remove the asterisks and underlining.

GARY GOLDING
291 Bayview
Seal Cove, ME 04674
(207) 622-1974

BACKGROUND
22 years in the construction business, from
framer to carpenter to general contractor.

* Proficient in all aspects of construction
from laying out footings with transit to the finish trim
* Experienced foreman and crew chief
* Skilled cabinet and woodworking craftsman
* Qualified in all types of custom laminating work

EXPERIENCE
GARY GOLDING CONSTRUCTION COMPANY, Seal Cove, ME (1982- present)

Owner of General Contracting business. Maintain an average work force of five employees. Handle a variety of jobs including:

• Complete renovation of 14 unit apartment building
• Renovation of retail furniture store
• Remodeling of French theme restaurant
• Remodeling and renovation of residential properties including patios, additions, dormers, cabinets and built-in wall units
• Specialize in building custom homes
• Built 8 homes in first 10 years in my own business

BILL BREWER CONTRACTING, Portsmouth, NH (1976- 1982)

Worked as Foreman and Lead Carpenter for a general contractor specializing in commercial and industrial construction. Examples of completed jobs are:

• A 40,000 square foot annex to a hospital building
• Total renovation of the main post office in Portsmouth
• New classroom wing of local middle school

EDUCATION
Coastal Community College
• Two years of night courses in Drafting, Design, and Blueprints

REFERENCES
Extensive references available from a wide range of clients

Note: The "background" is actually a "Qualifications Summary." Excellent use of specific examples throughout resume.

INGRID NATHANSON

118-A Coventry Street ▪ Brockton, MA ▪ (617) 363-2971

CAREER GOAL To secure a managerial position in sales or marketing.

CAREER SUMMARY 10 years of sales, marketing and supervisory experience, with a focus on printed and packaging materials. Skills in building direct and distributor business growth.

STRENGTHS
- Outstanding track record in sales and marketing
- Highly motivated and goal-oriented
- Excellent communication skills
- Skilled sales closer

EXPERIENCE

Sales Manager, Prime Packaging, Brockton, MA (1992-1995)
- Developed $4 million in new business.
- Initiated a line of custom boxes that generated more than $1 million in sales
- Managed a sales force of 10 representatives, in plant and on the road

Manufacturers of corrugated based promotional packaging, printed index tab dividers and custom file folders.

Sales Representative, Tab Products, Providence, Rl (1990-1992)
- One of the top 3 sales representatives nationally in percentage over quota: four consecutive years
- Over four years increased business from $485,000 per year to over $2 million per year (corporate average less than 10 percent per year growth)
- Coordinated a telemarketing program that was so successful that it was adopted nationally

Sales of Printed Index Tab Dividers: retail, wholesale, printing trade

Key Account Manager, Pawtucket Paper Products, Pawtucket, Rl (1987-1989)
- Increased sales from $19,000 monthly to $58,000 monthly in two years
- Responsibilities included establishing new accounts and servicing existing accounts

Paper Wholesaler selling to commercial printers

EDUCATION

Bachelor of Science Degree, Management
University of Connecticut, Storrs, CT 1987

Note: The section headed "Strengths" will certainly get an employer's attention. Ingrid describes each employer after she details her accomplishments.

IVAN G. INGERSOLL
22 Taylor Terrace
Brooklyn, NY 10551
(718) 694-1179

SUMMARY:
Experienced Director of Hotel Security seeks position in Western U.S.

EXPERIENCE:
The Algonquin, New York, NY
Director of Security, 6/91-Present
Developed security-related policies and procedures that have enhanced the hotel operation
Coordinated the security arrangements for visiting dignitaries, entertainers
and executives of Fortune 500 Companies
Responsible for Security and Fire Safety training of more than 200 hotel employees
Supervise staff of 15

The Ritz-Carlton, Boston, MA
Director of Security 2/86-6/91
Instituted, as well as restructured, security and safety policies for this exclusive 4-star hotel
Coordinator and liaison with government agencies for the security of visiting
international Heads of State and dignitaries
Supervised security measures for CEOs of Fortune 500 companies
Supervised and managed a department of 12 Security Officers and Timekeepers

The Helmsley Park, New York, NY
Assistant Director of Security 10/84-2/86
Hotel Assistant Manager 6/83-10/84
Security Officer 1/82-6/83

EDUCATION:
City University of New York, New York, NY
Bachelor of Science Degree, Criminal Justice

REFERENCES:
Available upon request.

Please respect the confidentiality of this resume.

Note: Ivan relies on his most recent jobs, both at well-known hotels, to secure interviews in a new geographical region.

Jennifer Wu
Dental Hygienist
1220 Olivia Street
Key West, FL 33040
(305) 294-2291

QUALIFICATIONS:

Skilled dental hygienist. Good rapport with dentists and patients. Specialty in periodontics. Expertise in all areas of general practice dentistry. Knowledgeable in office procedures. Devoted to patient education.

EXPERIENCE:

Dental Hygienist (1992–Present) Roberta Alomar, D.D.S., Periodontist, Key West, FL

> Perform oral prophylaxis.
> Place and remove periodontal dressings.
> Take and develop x-rays.
> Record patient histories.
> *Note: Dr. Alomar is relocating her practice to Colorado in the spring of 1995*

Dental Hygienist (1990–1992) Emily Jenkins, D.D.S., General Dentistry, Columbia, SC

> Performed all dental hygienist functions in busy office.

Office Assistant (1988–1990) Wendall Franklin, D.D.S., General Dentistry, Chapel Hill, NC

> Part-time position in front office of solo practitioner. Learned administrative functions of office, including scheduling, billing, insurance, etc.

EDUCATION:

> College of Medicine & Dentistry
> University of North Carolina, Chapel Hill, NC
> Periodontal Certification 1990
> Dental Hygiene Certification 1988
> Appalachian State University, Boone, NC, Attended 1985–1987

PERSONAL:

> Volunteer hygienist at Cayo Hueso Free Clinic, Key West

Note: The "Qualifications" section is an outstanding feature of this resume. It will gain a dentist's attention.

Kalle G. Xavier
41927 Skyline Drive
Topanga, CA 90290
(213) 683-2319

OBJECTIVE
Conscientious, detail-oriented recent graduate seeking position as Paralegal or Legal Secretary.

EDUCATION
A.A.S., Legal Studies, Santa Monica City College, December 1995

Dean's List; GPA 3.5

Extensive computer experience with WordPerfect 5.1 and Lotus 1-2-3

Relevant coursework includes:

Domestic Relations	Civil Litigation
Survey of Torts	Business Law 1 & 11
Legal Research & Writing	Wills & Probate
Real Estate Transactions	Corps. & Partnerships

EXPERIENCE
Intern, WomanCenter, Santa Monica, CA 9/95-12/95
- Counseled abused women on their legal rights and prerogatives.
- Accompanied clients to court.
- Interacted with judges on selected cases.

City of Los Angeles Police Department 11/89 - 11/94
Technical Assistant- Health Benefits Section
- Counseled active employees on their health benefits and plan options.
- Developed expertise in language and details of forms for various health plans.
- Extensive telephone contact and computer operations.
- Skilled in dictation and word processing.
- Promoted to Technical Assistant from Senior Clerk.

INTERESTS
Competitive rider and trainer in dressage. Have won three ribbons in regional (Western States) competition.

REFERENCES
Available on request.

Note: Willing to travel or relocate

Note: Kalle went back to school while she was employed. Like any recent graduate she emphasizes her relevant coursework and treats her internship like a job.

KENT ZELINKA
c/o Zelinka
2903-B Kuaui Road
Honolulu, HI 96816
(808)982-2873

OBJECTIVE
Naval Flight Officer seeks civilian position in organization that requires skills in management and supervision—and values capable, level-headed leadership.

MILITARY EXPERIENCE / UNITED STATES NAVY
Lieutenant, Assistant Air Department Officer
Naval Air Warfare Center, Honolulu, HI (January 1990 - December 1995)

Responsible for air operations, aviation support equipment maintenance, computer security and staff training. Supervised 25 air traffic controllers, 15 equipment maintenance technicians, and 10 aircraft line handlers.
- Reduced staffing by 35% with no loss in operational capability
- Reduced cost of aircraft maintenance by 25%
- Oversaw transition to new computer system

Ensign, Lieutenant Junior Grade
Naval Air Preparedness Center, Norfolk, VA (March 1987 - December 1989)

Navigator/Communicator and tactical coordinator.
Selected as Squadron Readiness Officer by superiors.
- Shaped 130 personnel into 11 fully capable aircrews ready for deployment
- Had sole responsibility for qualifying, training and scheduling all 11 crews.

Naval Flight Officer Training
San Diego, CA; Brunswick, ME; Pensacola, FL (August 1986 - February 1987)

Successfully completed prestigious 18-month training program, which included more than 50 sorties in actual flight as well as simulations in 6 different Navy and Air Force aircraft.

EDUCATION
B.S., Aeronautics & Aeronautical Engineering, 1986
University of South Carolina, Charleston, S.C.
- Naval ROTC scholarship for last 3 years of college
- Phi Eta Sigma national scholastic honor society, elected member
- Top 10% of Naval ROTC class
- Sigma Chi fraternity, Chapter President 1985-86

Note: Excellent use of "facts and figures" throughout resume. Good example of how to treat military experience as work experience.

LAWRENCE NANGLE
17 1/2 Foothill Road
Idaho Falls, ID 83402
(208) 876-1752

CAREER SUMMARY

Skilled salesperson with extensive experience in freight shipping. Strong record in acquiring and servicing new accounts. Outstanding customer relations skills.

EMPLOYMENT HISTORY

Account Manager, InterMountain Freight, Idaho Falls, ID (1994-present)
- Increased sales over 57% from 1993 to 1995
- Manage 175 to 200 accounts
- Give sales presentations to and interact with present and prospective customers
- Consistently one of top performers in region

Account Manager, Western Transport, Pocatello, ID (1992-1993)
- Managed 200 to 250 accounts in five states
- Strong in customer interaction, dealing well with clients on a one-to-one basis
- Resolved claims and service problems
- Acquired at least 50 new accounts
Note: Western Transport closed Pocatello terminal in November 1991

Outbound Supervisor, Domino Trucking, Las Vegas, NV (1991-1992)
- Supervised dock crew to properly load road trailers
- Kept track of dock production of each crew member
- Held conferences with workers who needed training or discipline
- Held safety meetings with all workers

Inbound Supervisor, Domino Trucking, Las Vegas, NV (1989-1991)
- Supervised dock crew to properly unload road trailers
- Maintained proper level of discipline and order on dock at all times
Note: This position was part-time while I completed college

EDUCATION

B.S., Physical Education
University of Nevada - Las Vegas

PERSONAL Speak conversational Spanish. Regularly use computers on the job.

Note: Larry has captured the key responsibilities of each job in his short, clear statements. The resume layout nicely emphasizes the bulleted points.

MADHURI PUNJABI   173 Maple Street
Lawrence, KS 66044
(913) 874-1998 Home
(913) 874-2382 Office

POSITION DESIRED: BOOK PRODUCTION DIRECTOR

SKILLS & QUALIFICATIONS

- *Recognized as an effective negotiator and decision maker*
- *Rewarded for consistently reducing production costs by 20-40%*
- *Thoroughly knowledgeable about book publishing and manufacturing techniques*
- *Experienced with all aspects of trade, college, reference, and art books*
- *Able to manage complex projects from initial design concept through final production*
- *Persistent, thorough, and prompt in completing projects, meeting deadlines, and staying within estimated costs*
- *Enthusiastic, energetic worker, excellent in a team setting*
- *Capable supervisor with strong people skills*

WORK EXPERIENCE
Production Manager
University Press of Kansas, Lawrence, KS 1991 - present

- *Responsible for the entire production process for art and archaeology books, as well as other heavily illustrated books: approximately 20 titles per year*
- *Negotiate contracts and bids with overseas and U.S. suppliers, constantly evaluating their performance*
- *Prepare production budgets for every book*
- *Administer effective quality control, cost containment and scheduling in the management of complex museum quality art books*
- *Effectively negotiate purchases, often resulting in $5,000 - $25,000 in savings*
- *Develop liaisons with manufacturers, in-house personnel, editors, sales, marketing, and free-lance designers*

Production Manager, W.W. Norton, New York, NY 1984 - 1991

Reprint Manager, Basic Books, New York, NY 1982 - 1984

EDUCATION

M.A., English Literature, University of Calcutta

Certificate, Book Production, University of Pennsylvania

U.S. Citizen since 1981

Note: Terrific use of skills and qualifications, nicely blended together. Wise note about citizenship.

MARGARET EARLY
221-B Merchant Green • Ann Arbor, MI 48104 • (517) 637-9210

OBJECTIVE: A position leading to a career in finance

EDUCATION

M.B.A., Finance, University of Michigan, Expected June 1997
B.S., With highest honors, University of Minnesota, June 1992

PERSONAL PROFILE

Exposure to various aspects of business, including finance, accounting, human resources, marketing and merchandising. Special talent for using innovative and resourceful methods in problem solving, time management and planning. Adaptable, able to learn quickly.

PROFESSIONAL SKILLS

Management: Interviewed, hired and trained staff. Responsible for all aspects of operating retail store.
Analysis: Monitored inventory stock levels, selling and merchandise trends to make purchasing decisions and optimize business profits.
Budgeting: Analyzed monthly department spending as related to targeted budget. Created spreadsheets to organize data and compute information for presentation.
Marketing: Coordinated monthly fashion shows and promotions which generated business and improved customer relations.
Communication: Excellent selling techniques and ability to communicate with people, as well as outstanding writing skills.
Computer: Proficient in Lotus, WordPerfect, and FoxPro. Provided spreadsheet support for various departments in Technical Operations.

PROFESSIONAL ACHIEVEMENTS

Enhanced Training: Developed a training program to enhance employee product knowledge and selling skills which was adopted by stores throughout the company. Placed 60% of my store staff into managerial positions.
Increased Productivity: Created store contests and meetings to motivate staff and maintain standards of customer service, resulting in a 30% increase in annual sales.
Improved Customer Service: Awarded "Outstanding Retailer" by Main Place Mall for excellence in customer service. Received annual Productivity Award from corporate office.

EMPLOYMENT HISTORY

Senior Assistant to Director of Human Resources, W.K. Kellogg, BattleCreek, MI (July 1994 - Present)
Manager, Jeans Plus, Main Place Mall, St. Paul, MN (December 1992 - June 1994)
Began as clerk while in college and progressed to Assistant Manager upon graduation. Appointed manager within six months.

Note: Meg put a lot of effort into identifying and grouping her skills and achievements. The effort was certainly worthwhile.

NANCY GARCIA
8915 Saguaro Way
Maricopa, Arizona 85239
(602) 292-1714

OBJECTIVE
Seeking day-shift position in nursing

EXPERIENCE

Staff Nurse, Medical/Surgical Floor
Desert Center Hospital, Maricopa, Arizona

Staff Nurse, Oncology
Desert Center Hospital, Maricopa, Arizona

Licensed Practical Nurse
Hot Springs Nursing Home, Hot Springs, Arizona

EDUCATION

Enrolled in R.N. Certificate Program
Maricopa Community College

Associate's Degree in Nursing
Maricopa Community College

Licensed Practical Nurse Certification
Hot Springs Area Education Center

PERSONAL

President, Parent-Teacher Association, Hernando Soto Elementary School
Volunteer, American Cancer Society, Southern Chapter
Assistant Scoutmaster, Girl Scout Troop #153

REFERENCES

Angelina Hernandez, Nursing Supervisor, Hot Springs Nursing Home (602) 791-1812

Evelyn Katonah, M.D., Director, On-Call Emergency Care Center (602) 864-8227

Fay Ohnuki, Principal, Hernando Soto Elementary School (602) 793-2318

Note: Here is a working mother, who has worked both full and part-time and gone back to school. Dates would only be confusing. She works in a field that requires references.

ORLANDO TITUS
11 Nottingham Drive
Duluth, MN 55807
(218) 892-9312

CAREER SUMMARY:
More than 10 years of experience designing and implementing user friendly software applications for laboratory process control, data acquisition, data analysis and data display on large scale projects. Work with extreme accuracy under pressure.

HARDWARE EXPERIENCE:	VAX Family, SUN Workstations, Gould
OPERATING SYSTEMS:	VMS, UNIX, MPX
LANGUAGES:	FORTRAN, C, IDL
SOFTWARE:	INGRES, SQL

WORK EXPERIENCE:
APPLICATIONS ENGINEER, Physical Systems, Inc., Duluth, MN 1987 - present
Responsible for the design, implementation and maintenance of software applications using real-time control, data acquisition, data analysis and graphics for major physics projects measuring extreme densities and temperatures.
- Interfaced with end-user physicists, hardware engineers and systems programmers from initial requirements, design and implementation through maintenance and enhancements
- Served as Engineer-in-Charge to field questions and problems of physicists during experiments.
- Diagnosed and solved hardware and software problems
- Provided orientation and support to contract programmers

PROGRAMMER/ANALYST, Southwest Oil Services, Durango, CO 1982 - 1987
Primary duties involved the design and implementation of software used in oil exploration.
- Designed and implemented database and graphics programs used by management and scientists as their major software tool
- Designed and implemented process control software of automated test systems measuring spectral responses of photomultiplier tubes under computer controlled conditions

EDUCATION
Bachelor of Science, University of Arizona, Tucson, AZ 1981
Major: Computer Science   Minor: Earth and Environmental Sciences

PERSONAL
- Worked my way around the world on oil tankers after graduating from college
- Volunteer computer teacher in school district's "Professionals in the Classroom" program

Note: The use of technical jargon is to be expected from a software designer. The "personal section" helps to humanize him a little.

Quentin C. Goodman

319 Greenleaf Road • Fort Wayne, IN 46804 • (812) 594-2312

OBJECTIVE:

Fitness counselor in a corporate facility where experience in the health field and human sciences will be utilized by an employer to enhance corporate goals.

PERSONAL PROFILE

Experienced in fitness environment; skilled in customizing general programs and equipment to meet the needs of individuals. Self-directed with proven leadership and decision-making skills, as well as ability to learn fast and follow directions. People skills with strong ability in written and oral communication as well as one-on-one and group instruction. Organized and detail-oriented.

PROFESSIONAL SKILLS

Instruction: Created and instructed an aerobic interval training class which encompassed five pieces of fitness apparatus to improve cardiovascular fitness.
Diagnostic Testing: Interacted with cardiac diagnostic team of major medical center. Experience included exposure to stress testing, echocardiographic analysis, and exercise prescription.
Communication: Lectured corporate staff in wellness-oriented subjects such as lower back care, nutrition and hypertension.
Management: Supervised daily activities of Fitness Center including maintenance of equipment, administrative tasks, and interfacing with office and medical staff.
Organization: Involved in establishment of NCR Fitness Center, which entailed designing promotional material, field testing, supervising and evaluating performance of participants.

EDUCATION

B.S., Corporate Fitness, Wayne State University, September, 1989 to May 1994. Related courses: Anatomy & Physiology I & 11, Exercise Physiology, Kinesiology, Nutrition, General Biology I & II, and Fitness in Business & Industry.

EMPLOYMENT HISTORY

Fitness Center Supervisor
May 1992 to August 1992

NCR Corporation
Manufacturing Firm

Fitness Assistant
August 1991

Pro Fitness
Corporate Fitness Consulting Firm

Cardiac Rehabilitation Assistant
Internship - May 1990 to August 1991

St. Thomas Medical Center
Cardiac Rehabilitation Unit

Note: "Personal Profile" mixes skills and qualifications, while "Professional Skills" includes accomplishments. An excellent resume by a recent graduate.

RAMONA ALVAREZ, A.C.S.W.
Clinical Social Worker
1142 Wayland Ave.
Louisville, KY 40210
Office: (502) 799-3535
Answering Service: (502) 794-2996

CERTIFICATIONS	Certified Board Diplomate in Clinical Social Work, 1991 N.A.S.W. Diplomate in Clinical Social Work, 1989 A.C.S.W., 1985
EDUCATION	M.S.W., Social Casework Concentration University of Kentucky, Louisville, KY 1983 B.A., Sociology, Berea College, Berea, KY, 1981

EXPERIENCE
Director of Clinical Services
CATHOLIC FAMILY SERVICES
Louisville, KY 1992 - present

Oversee all clinical programs including personal counseling, suicide prevention, family abuse mediation, community outreach, and substance abuse treatment.

• Supervise staff of 8 full-time and 4 part-time M.S.W. social workers
• Supervise 5 support staff and paraprofessionals
• Supervise 4-6 graduate student interns

Clinical Director
THE CRISIS CENTER
Louisville, KY 1989 - 1992
• Supervised all-volunteer staff at 24-hour crisis "hotline"
• Responsible for training and scheduling staff of more than 80 hotline counselors

Previous experience includes social work positions with public and private agencies in several cities within Kentucky

PERSONAL
• Placed 3rd in 1994 10-mile "Fun Run" sponsored by Louisville Charities Council
• Volunteer coach of the "Hurricanes" pee-wee soccer team

Note: In a field where certifications and education are significant, Ramona lists these first. She focuses on her most recent experience and assumes that she will discuss her first eight years of work when she interviews.

Roberta B. Nadel   433 Aspen Road   Boulder, CO 80304   (303) 797-8314

OBJECTIVE
Seeking challenging position in the field of Drug and Alcohol Counseling, Testing, Interviewing, or Research

EDUCATION
B.A., Psychology, May 1995
University of Colorado, Boulder, CO

EXPERIENCE
Volunteer, Project HELP, Boulder, CO June, 1995 - Present

Intake worker for people living with AIDS.
Includes interviewing to assess risk taking behavior, personal stability, apparent level of distress and service needs. Provide crisis counseling and crisis intervention on an as-needed basis and assist in obtaining entitlements, health care, housing and other services.

Intern, Boulder House, Boulder, CO January - May, 1995

Counselor at general psychiatric/alcohol and drug abuse treatment facility.
Worked in Dual Diagnosis program under direction of Psychiatric Social Worker:
- Facilitated adjunctive therapy groups.
- Conducted some one-to-one counseling sessions.
- Participated in daily Dual Diagnosis Meetings.
- Attended daily General Staff Meetings.
- Completed billing and patient charting.
- Helped set up aftercare.
- Followed-up on aftercare arrangements after discharge.

INDEPENDENT STUDY
Diabetes Clinic - Boulder Medical Center, Boulder, CO. 1/95 - 5/95
Researched coping skills of adolescents with insulin-dependent diabetic mellitus and their parents. Observed patients' and families' behavior.

Rocky Mountain Psychiatric Hospital, Boulder, CO. 1/94 - 5/94
Facility treating Mentally Ill/Chemically Addictive (MICA) patients. Designed and developed interview forms for research project on treatment plans for dual diagnosis patients. Interviewed patients and staff about dual treatment plan.

Note: Here is an entire resume without paid work experience. Notice how Roberta has treated her unpaid experience just as if it were a "real" job.

SHERI MENDEL
84 Creek Road
Missoula, MT 59806
(406) 751 - 1953

GOAL

Seeking part-time position as medical assistant. Special expertise in management of diabetes. Excellent interpersonal skills.

EDUCATIONAL QUALIFICATIONS

Western Montana Community College
Medical Assistant Training Program
Graduated 1995
Montana State University
B.S., Biology, 1980

Most recent training included:

ADMINISTRATIVE:
- scheduling
- medical records management
- medical transcription
- accounting/billing
- patient relations

CLINICAL
- medical histories
- laboratory procedures
- taking vital signs
- sterilizing instruments
- patient education

Certified Medical Assistant
Member, American Association of Medical Assistants

BACKGROUND

American Diabetes Association
- President, Diabetes Association of Missoula (local chapter)
  Served two terms: 1986-1988; 1990-1992
- Delegate to state association from Missoula chapter, 1989-1990

- Have lectured throughout western part of state on diabetes and insulin management
- Have attended numerous workshops on diabetes

PERSONAL

Single parent of teenage diabetic child. Able to work up to 30 hours per week.

Note: Sheri has completed a training program after 15 years of working in the home and as a volunteer. Her son was severely diabetic when he was younger. Her resume makes the most of her recent training and her volunteer work.

TANYA YOUNG
11954 Silverado, Apt. 3, Phoenix, AZ 85016 (602) 493-1337

QUALIFICATIONS
Experienced sportswear and accessories buyer who has consistently exceeded sales goals. Knowledgeable in all aspects of retail clothing store operations and purchasing.

EXPERIENCE
Buyer, Sportswear
FASHIONS WEST, Phoenix, AZ (Corporate Headquarters) 1994 - present
Function:
• Responsible for all aspects of buying and merchandising sportswear for chain of 15 stores with annual sales volume over $4 million
Accomplishments:
• Generated a 25% increase in sportswear sales in two years
• Increased sportswear sales from 70-80% of total company's sales volume in two years
• Worked closely with manufacturers to develop exclusive merchandise for stores
• Planned, purchased for and attended new store openings
• Developed sportswear sales plans for all 15 stores

Manager
CAREER CORNER, Tucson, AZ 1991 - 1994
Function:
• Managed a $2 million retail clothing store
Accomplishments:
• Hired, trained and developed staff of eight
• Increased sales by more than 10% per year
• Maintained high level of communication with own staff members and upper management to ensure company objectives were met

Assistant Buyer
I.MAGNIN, Los Angeles, CA 1989 - 1991
Function:
• Active partner in coordinating procurement, store distribution and seasonal sales/stock plans
Accomplishments:
• Purchased more than $10 million per year in sportswear and accessories
• Projected seasonal advertising plans by determining advertisement strategies in each geographic market and determined productivity of advertisements through analysis of computerized retail buying records

EDUCATION
SYRACUSE UNIVERSITY
Bachelor of Science Degree
Retailing & Marketing   Grade point average in major: 3.6 (on 4.0 scale)

Note: Tanya outlines her function and accomplishments for her most recent jobs in a very appealing way.

Terese B. Ellermann

112 Shore Drive
Dover, DE 19901
(302) 979-6388

OBJECTIVE

A product development position which will utilize my technical design skills in electrical engineering.

WORK EXPERIENCE

Product Development Engineer

Fluortech, Inc. January, 1994- Present

Work to develop state-of-the-art fluorescent lamp ballasts for small start-up company. Develop products from the conceptual stage to the production level.

Responsible for:
- Circuit design and documentation
- Component specification and sourcing
- PCB Design
- UL listing procedures and quality procedures
- Resolving quality issues
- Managing six-terminal LAN system

TECHNICAL EXPERIENCE

CAD for schematics, PCB layout and auto-routing, AutoCAD
LANtastic Network OS and related hardware
Pascal, BASIC, Assembly languages for TMS320C25, 8088, 8051, PSPICE and Microcap simulation programs

EDUCATION

University of Delaware
Bachelor of Science, January, 1994
Major: Electrical Engineering

Designed Voice Recognition System using TMS320 DSP chip. Researched speech theory and recognition algorithms for use in assembly program. (Senior Project, January - December, 1993)

Note: Terri has had only one job, but she has clearly spelled out her responsibilities and her technical knowledge.

ULANDA HART
7184-A Heron Parkway
Little Rock, Arkansas 72206
(501) 882-2319

OBJECTIVE   Hard-working college graduate with degree in accounting wants
                   to make a contribution to the financial health of a bank or business.

EXPERIENCE
        Little Rock Savings Bank, Little Rock, AR
Bank Reconciliation Technician 6/92- present
  Reconcile investor custodial accounts
  Research inquiries from mortgagors and investors regarding disbursements
  Initiate wire transfer of funds between savings bank and Federal Home Loan Bank
  Investigate foreclosure loss at loan level basis, enabling management to make
  proper account entry decisions

Cash Technician (part-time position) 1/91-6/92
  Reconciled foreclosure loss reserve accounts
  Prepared Real Estate Owned reports for presentation to Board of Directors
  Processed payoffs, regular installment payments and foreclosure settlements

        University of Arkansas, Little Rock, AR 6/89-9/89
Bookkeeper, Council of Student Organizations
  Paid part-time accounting position
  Dispersed more than $500,000 in student funds
  Wrote all checks requested by more than 75 student organizations

EDUCATION
University of Arkansas, Little Rock, AR
Degree: Bachelor of Science, June 1990
Major: Accounting   G.P.A.: 3.56 (on a 4.0 sscale)
        Note: Self-financed 80% of cost of education

SKILLS
Lotus 1-2-3; Quattro; Paradox; Data Base 111; Wordstar: Professional Write

ACTIVITIES
National Association of Accountants (Student Member) 1990-1992
Delta Delta Delta Sorority 1989-1992, Treasurer 1991-1992

REFERENCES
Available upon request

*Note: Ulanda makes the most of her limited experience and keeps the resume
focused on accounting and finance.*

UNA S. UNDERWOOD   815 Summit Road
Juneau, AK 99850
(907) 331-8956

SUMMARY

Over 5 years experience installing, troubleshooting, administrating,developing, implementing and training with IBM/PC's in a Local Area Network Token Ring Architecture and with Wang's PC's in a Wide Area Network

ACCOMPLISHMENTS

ADMINISTRATION

• Administered, planned and maintained a Local Area Network made up of IBM PS/2's on an OS/2 Token Ring
• In charge of distributing and maintaining all computer equipment for office
• Delivered, installed, and provided maintenance on networked PC's, mainframes, and software for 120 legislative district offices, eliminating the need for a $250K maintenance contract

DEVELOPMENT

• Developed interface between Auditor's office PC LAN and the Legislature's Bill Tracking and Statute Retrieval System, improving auditor efficiency
• Developed and implemented an inventory and resume database used by peer review for annual certification
• Improved productivity by developing and implementing a project management system

TECHNICAL

Hardware	Token Ring LAN Architecture using IBM PS/2's, Wang Systems
Software	WordPerfect, Multimate, Quattro Pro, E-Mail, Lotus 1-2-3, dBase, Alpha 4, SAS
Operating Systems	OS/2, MS-DOS, JCL

EXPERIENCE

State of Alaska, State Auditor's Office, Juneau, AK
   Auditor, 12/92 - Present
State of Alaska, Office of Legislative Services, Juneau, AK
   PC User Consultant, 7/89 - 12/92

EDUCATION

University of Alaska, Juneau, AK
   BS in Business Administration Major: Accounting, 1989 - 1992
Sheldon Jackson College, Sitka, AK 1988 - 1989

Note: Una divides her accomplishments into three separate categories and then lists her employment history under the heading of "Experience."

XAVIER FREDERICK
31275 Baltimore Pike Bowie, MD 20720 (410) 597-2279

OBJECTIVE: Seeking responsible position in corporate security. Offering extensive experience and education.

EXPERIENCE:

Senior Correction Officer, Maryland State Correctional Facility (1995-present)
* Control Post Officer with detail of approximately 30 officers, overseeing access to four major areas
* Procure supplies, issue job assignments and supervise inmate workers in their assigned tasks.
* Maintain monthly payroll and rating system for employees, including weekly updates.
* Perform various other custody functions including inmate and area searches, maintaining discipline, and control of contraband.
* Perform investigations on inmate infractions and issue disciplinary reports
* Supervise up to three officers in conducting investigations

Senior Correction Officer, Baltimore County Youth Home (1987-1989)
* Housing Officer in charge of approximately 20 juveniles on an assigned shift
* Maintained custody and control of juveniles while also safeguarding their well-being and attending to their individual needs

EDUCATION:

Pursuing B.S. in Administration of Justice, Bowie State College
Degree expected, June 1996
A.A.S. Corrections, Community College of Baltimore, (1990)

MILITARY:

Operations Officer, U.S. Army, Berlin, Germany (1992-1995)
* Responsible for developing, producing, acquiring and supporting weapons systems, ammunition, missiles and ground mobility material during peace and war.
* Comprehensive knowledge of maintenance management, production control and quality assurance

Officer Candidate School, Quantico, VA
* Commissioned Officer, 2nd Lieutenant, September 1, 1992

REFERENCES: Excellent personal and professional references available upon request.

PLEASE MAINTAIN THE CONFIDENTIALITY OF THIS RESUME.

Note: Xavier's military service comes between his two jobs but he groups the related work together and handles military service in its own section.

CATHERINE M. YANG
12235 34th St., Apt. 3-G
Chicago, IL 60612
(312) 674-2932 (Office)
(312) 976-7413 (Home)

SUMMARY

Award-winning copywriter
  Work effectively as team member
  Relate well to clients
  Skilled in research techniques
  Manage photographers, graphic designers, media planners,
  and production personnel
  Develop effective advertising, marketing, and p.r. campaigns

EXPERIENCE

General Foods (print ads) Pioneer Audio (package design) Westside Electronics (newspaper ads) Mita Copiers (collateral materials) Chicago City College (magazine, newspaper, transit ads) Chicago Museum of Art (direct mail campaign awarded first place in competition with all museums in Illinois)

EMPLOYMENT

Megacom (ad agency) Chicago, IL
  Senior copywriter
Smith, Coverdale (ad agency) Chicago, IL
  Copywriter
Clovis and Maven (ad agency) Chicago, IL
  Copywriter

EDUCATION

B.A., English, Lake Forest College, Lake Forest, IL
Participant, "Shakespeare Semester," Stratford-on-Avon, England

PERSONAL

Volunteer Director, Southside Children's Theater, Chicago

Drama coach/director at inner city theater program for disadvantaged youth

Note: Advertising-industry resumes concentrate on accounts and campaigns.
Their design can be unusual. Dates are not essential.

Anita Ramone
c/o Elite Talent Management
11925 Peachtree Road • Atlanta, GA 30318 • (404) 977-3422

TELEVISION:

"Days of Our Lives": Waitress (speaking part)
"Santa Barbara": Nurse (walk-on)
"Beverly Hills 90210": Secretary (non-speaking)

NATIONAL ADVERTISING:

Atlanta Braves: Fan (close-up)
Georgia Tourism Board: Vendor (speaking)

LOCAL ADVERTISING:

15 appearances to date including 10 speaking parts. Featured parts in commercials for Peachtree Spa, Doubletree Hotels, and Calhoun Nissan.

NATIONAL FILM:

"Doc Hollywood": patient (non-speaking)
"My Cousin Vinny": courtroom spectator (non-speaking)

VIDEO:

21 appearances to date in industrial videos. Featured parts in 5 videos, including narrator for "Our Georgia: Welcome To It" produced for Georgia Tourism Board (on-screen speaking and overdubbed narration).

TALENTS:

Read and speak Spanish
Excellent with accents. Can do inflected English, with Spanish, French, and Italian accents.
Face and hands used extensively in close-ups.
Can portray numerous ethnicities
Good with children of all ages
Good with all kinds of animals
Play piano, flute, violin, viola

Can travel. Available on short notice.

Note: This is a typical resume for an actress. The focus in on "appearances." A photo accompanies the resume.

CURRICULUM VITAE
Kanesha Turner
University of Missouri   Department of English
Columbia, MO 65202   (314) 767-9734

PRESENT POSITION
Assistant Professor of English, University of Missouri, 1994 - Present

EDUCATION
Ph.D., English, University of Georgia, Athens, GA 1991
    Dissertation: "The Dark Side of The Moonstone: Tragedy and Melodrama
    in the Works of Wilkie Collins"
M.A., English, University of Georgia 1989
B.A., English, Spelman College, Atlanta, GA 1985
    Graduated with honors
    Distinction in senior thesis

TEACHING EXPERIENCE
Visiting Adjunct Instructor of English, Georgia Southwestern College,
    Americus, GA 1992 - 94
Courses included: Composition 1, Introduction to English Literature,
Introduction to the Victorian Novel

Teaching Assistant, University of Georgia, 1987 - 92
Courses included: Composition, Advanced Composition, Honors Composition,
Introduction to Literature, English Literature: An Introduction,
The Victorians, Introduction to the Victorian Novel

ADMINISTRATIVE EXPERIENCE
Coordinator, Freshman Composition Program, University of Georgia 1990 - 92
Elected representative to faculty senate, Graduate Student Association, 1989

PUBLICATIONS
"The Dark Side of The Moonstone: Tragedy and Melodrama in the Works of Wilkie
    Collins," accepted for editorial review by University of California Press and
    University of Chicago Press
"Tragedy Meets Melodrama: Wilkie Collins and The Moonstone,"
    19th-Century Literature, Vol. 10, 2, Summer 1995
"Melodrama and Tragedy in Victorian Novels," published as chapter in
    Teaching the Victorian Novel (University of Minnesota Press, 1994)

LANGUAGES
French: reading proficiency, writing proficiency, speaking fluency
German: reading proficiency   Spanish: speaking proficiency

*Note: This is a "vita." Kanesha is typical of a professor early in a career.
The section entitled "Administrative Experience" is a smart addition to the vita.*

CARL UNWYN

120 Spur Circle
Houston, TX 77020

(713) 592-2312

SUMMARY

Offering over 12 years' experience in the Information Systems and Telecommunications industry: 5 years in technical training and 7 years directly dealing with customer support and equipment maintenance

QUALIFICATIONS

Skilled teacher
Experienced engineer
Effective with clients, coworkers, and computers
Thorough knowledge of UNISYS product line
Productive in a variety of work settings

ACCOMPLISHMENTS

UNISYS CORPORATION, HOUSTON, TX

DEVELOPER/INSTRUCTOR (1988 -present)
   Responsible for the development and delivery of training for PC and Unix communications and network products
   Led team to develop a self-paced computer, video and text based training package which was accepted as corporate standard and used nationwide
   Developed and conducted more than 20 hardware classes on mainframes, mini's and PC's
   Developed and conducted more than 10 software classes on operating systems and applications

SENIOR SITE ENGINEER (1981-1988)
   Responsible for installation, maintenance, upgrade and repair for mainframes, peripherals and communications equipment 4 Increased installation efficiency by 15%, leading to improved customer satisfaction and decreased company costs
   Employed preventative maintenance procedures to maintain on-line site effeciency of 99.5%. This resulted in one of the lowest "down time" rates of any corporate field office

PLEASE SEE NEXT PAGE

CARL UNWYN
Page Two

MILITARY SERVICE: U.S. AIR FORCE (1973-1981)
Responsibilities included maintenance and repair of
airfield based and mobile communications, radar
and navigational equipment

EDUCATION   U.S. AIR FORCE Technical Training School
Associate Degree

TECHNICAL TRAINING   UNISYS Education Center, Houston, TX
UNIX Communications & Networking, 1992
UNIX Shell Programming, 1992
UNIX System Administration, 1992
Local Area Network Administration, 1990
1100/90 Advanced Troubleshooting, 1989
110/60 System Maintenance, 1988
Peripheral Theory & Repair, 1987
U1050 – II System Maintenance, 1985

SOFTWARE EXPERIENCE   LAN   Novell Netware 286
UNIX   System V.3, Shell, C, TCP/IP, UUCP, FTP, SMTP
PC   MS-DOS, Basic, C, dBase III, Clipper, Excell 2.1,
Word Perfect 5.1, Draw Perfect 1.1, Harvard Graphics
2.1, XyWrite III, Misc Utilities
Mainframe OS1100, ECL

HARDWARE EXPERIENCE   PC   Unisys - HT, JT, UIT, PW2 500
Communication Unisys - DCP40/20/10
Mainframe Unisys- 2200/600ES, 2200/600, 2200/400,
2200/200, 100/90, System ll/Mapper 10, 1100/60,1050-II
Peripheral Unisys - Disk: 8433, 8436, 8440, 8451, 8470
Unisys - Tape: U22/24, U26/28, U30/32, Steamer
Unisys – Printer: 770-II, 776, 789

---

*Note: Carl's resume is well-detailed and very specific. He devotes the first page
to catching attention and the second to technical specifications.*

CLAUDIA BATEMAN

2319 Valencia Drive
Tustin, California 92701
Home (714) 542-5796   Work (714) 639-2710

PROFESSIONAL OBJECTIVE

Position as a Learning Disability Teacher/Consultant

HIGHLIGHTS OF QUALIFICATIONS

- Over 15 years experience meeting educational needs of special students
- Committed to equal opportunities for all students
- Capable of working in varied settings
- Collaborate well with colleagues and administration

PROFESSIONAL EXPERIENCE

ASSESSMENT

- Evaluated students using varied assessment methods including:
  - standardized and criterion instruments
  - curriculum based assessment
  - diagnostic teaching
  - student and teacher interview
  - record review and classroom observation
- Assessed students presenting a diversity of educationally handicapping conditions including emotional disturbance, all levels of retardation, autism, multiple handicaps and learning difficulties.

COLLABORATIVE PROBLEM SOLVING

- Empowered teachers to develop more effective instruction to meet the needs of an extremely diverse student population.
- Obtained support and involvement from administrative, professional and non-professional staff to identify and address instructional challenges.

CASE MANAGEMENT

- Performed approximately 100 annual reviews and reclassifications in compliance with state and federal regulations.

CURRICULUM DEVELOPMENT

- Assisted in the development of a Curriculum Guide used in the educational facilities of the Department of Human Services.
- Researched and wrote curriculum for mental health course used with students in a psychiatric facility. Course spanned 3 years and involved 300 participants. Program was submitted by Department of Human Services to the American Psychiatric Association's Achievement Awards Competition.

CLAUDIA BATEMAN
Page 2

WORK EXPERIENCE

1992 - Present
- Learning Disability Teacher/Consultant
    - Serve as case manager for Douglas Training and Research Center and Naremore Development Center
    - Perform educational assessment for 8 local inpatient and outpatient psychiatric centers
    - Conduct per-case evaluations for private, public and parochial schools

1984 - 1992 Teacher, Frederick Psychiatric Hospital
- Full-time position working with students of all ages and backgrounds
- Implemented innovative peer reading program

1977 - 1984 Teacher, Special Education - various public school districts
- Experienced in T.M.R., Resource Room and Primary ED class
- Supervised para-professional assistants
- Developed reading programs

PROFESSIONAL CERTIFICATIONS
L.D.T.C. 1990
Teacher of the Handicapped 1977
Elementary Education 1977

EDUCATION
1990 University of Southern California, L.D.T.C. Certification Program
1988 University of Southern California - Course leading to Principal Certification
1982 M.A. University of Southern California, Special Education
1977 B.A. California State College, Fullerton, Major - English, Minor - Elementary Education

PROFESSIONAL ASSOCIATIONS
California Association for Learning Consultants
Council for Exceptional Children

REFERENCES
Will be furnished upon request

Note: Claudia first highlights her qualifications and experience and then details her employment and education.

Karen Trump   11921 Westend Avenue   (212) 979-2673
                             New York, NY 10012
                             Apartment 3-G

QUALIFICATIONS

Graphic artist skilled in the use of state-of-the-art technologies
Electronically "draw" images for computer animation
Create special effects in type and backgrounds for a nationally televised
home shopping service
Design storyboards on computer
Shoot, edit, and sound-edit short video footage
Utilize all traditional graphic arts in design of print materials

EXPERIENCE

Video Layout Artist, Electronic Media Department, Macy's, Inc.,
New York, NY (1993 - Present)

> Computer graphic artist for televised home shopping service
> Create still video screens (with type and images) for national
> broadcast
> Develop and implement procedures, techniques, and formats for adapting
> color catalog ektachromes to television medium
> Interact with printed catalog art staff as liaison from electronic
> catalog department

Senior Graphic Artist, Consumer Catalog Department, Macy's, Inc.,
New York, NY (1990 - 1993)

> Supervising layout artist for 4 major catalogs and 28 tabloids per year
> Designed layout and type specifications
> Interfaced with photographers and printers to ensure accurate and
> timely production of catalogs
> Created new design formats for publication

TECHNICAL

> Skilled in use of Macintosh computers and peripherals
> Skilled in use of numerous design software packages, including
> PageMaker, Studio 8, Quark Xpress, MacroMind Director, Type Styler and others
> Skilled in use of Colorgraphics Art Star 3D computer and peripherals

EDUCATION

> B.A., Fine Arts, New York University
> Continuing education courses at Parsons Institute of Design, New York City

*Note: Karen positions herself immediately with her qualifications. She has
been a graphic artist for many years but she does not indicate any dates
that might reveal her age.*

Michael Mendez
119-D Coventry Lane
Surfside, CA 90743
(707) 968-4923

SUMMARY   **Marketing Manager** skilled in all phases of marketing, with special strengths in catalog marketing and targeted direct-response marketing.

EXPERIENCE   **Marketing Manager** , Allcraft Publishing, San Luis Obispo, CA
- Increased sales volume by 15% in first year
- Reduced marketing expenses by 20% in first year through better targeting of catalog mailing
- Increased catalog sales by 30% in three years
- Increased overall response rates from 4% to 8%: a 100% jump in three years

Assistant Marketing Manager , Alessi Yarn Co.,
Los Angeles, CA
- Doubled income from direct-to-consumer marketing
- Initiated first consumer advertising campaign
- Supervised transition from black-and-white to four-color catalogs for wholesalers, retailers, and consumers

Assistant Marketing Manager , Wonderland Looms, Duluth, MN

Sales Representative , Wonderland Looms, Duluth, MN

EDUCATION   Bachelor of Business Administration
University of Iowa, Iowa City, IA
Major: Marketing   Minor: Advertising

PERSONAL   Volunteer tutor at La Raza Community Center,
San Luis Obispo, CA
Volunteer speaker in local program: "Education Means Jobs"

Note: As a marketing manager, Mike concentrates on his tangible results in his two most recent jobs.

Alice Mojica

733 Tudor Road
Anchorage, Alaska 99503
(907) 743-1437

PROFILE

- ❑ Hard working, conscientious Physician Assistant, skilled at putting people at ease and inspiring confidence in the physician, treatment, and the practice
- ❑ Well-versed in the Managed Health Care environment
- ❑ Knowledgeable with medical billing and patient management software
- ❑ Demonstrated leader as well as team member
- ❑ Able to function under stress and within short time frames

EXPERIENCE

Physician Assistant

Lisa Gaffney, M.D., Anchorage, Alaska

- ❑ Takes medical history and performs physical examinations for a family practice in internal medicine with over 8000 active files
- ❑ Treats lacerations, abrasions and burns
- ❑ Makes preliminary diagnoses, carries out appropriate treatment, performs phlebotom and orders required lab tests
- ❑ Answers questions about treatments and procedures in order to put patients at ease
- ❑ Assists with minor in-office surgery, OB-GYN examinations, performs cardiograms and administers immunizations
- ❑ Performs chemistries with biodynamics reagents using spectrometrics methods
- ❑ Handles insurance billing using Signature software
- ❑ Pays bills, orders supplies and maintains records

Physician Assistant to Dermatologist (Part Time)

Providence Hospital, Anchorage, Alaska

- ❑ Screened calls in order to determine severity and scheduled appointments depending on need
- ❑ Assisted the Dermatologist within a Managed Health Care environment
- ❑ Conferred with patients, answered inquiries and provided information over the telephone

EDUCATION

University of Alaska, Anchorage, Alaska
Physician Assistant Program

University of Alaska, Fairbanks, Alaska
Major in Math and Science

City University of New York
Major in Elementary Education and Science

Member of American Association of Medical Assistants

Note: Alice describes herself in the "Profile" section in a way that will make a prospective employer keep reading. She knows what employers need and she speaks directly to their needs.

Bernadette Galloway

41 Lafayette Drive • Oxford, MS 38655 • (601) 977-3669

OBJECTIVE

A Social Services position in which I can apply counseling, administrative and communications skills.

COUNSELING

▮ Counseled adolescents with behavioral problems, helping them change their behaviors
▮ Tutored and conducted workshops to improve academic performance of clients
▮ Counseled adolescents in alcohol and drug related matters

CASE MANAGEMENT

▮ Assessed the needs of clients through patience and employing a process of "talking to, not at"
▮ Put together the most appropriate package of services in consultation with client and providers
▮ Followed through with providers to assure that the needed services were delivered

ADMINISTRATION

▮ Assisted in processing applications for naturalization including fingerprinting, photographing, and verifying client information
▮ Handled payments and maintained accounts
▮ Implemented civil rights policies throughout organization

COMMUNICATIONS

▮ Listened to concerns of clients, creating a climate of openness and trust to develop solutions
▮ Assisted in writing civil rights guidelines in compliance with federal regulations
▮ Responded to inquiries regarding immigration issues from clients; drafted letters and forms

EDUCATION

Jackson State University, Jackson, MS   May 1995
B.A. Degree in Sociology with a Criminal Justice/Juvenile Delinquency concentration

EXPERIENCE

Currently employed at University of Mississippi Office of the General Counsel, Oxford, MS, 6/95-present

Intern - Jackson Police Department, Jackson, MS, 1/95-5/95
Program Specialist - United States Department of Agriculture, Jackson, MS, Summer 1994
Legal Assistant - Immigration Law Center, Jackson, MS, Summers 1991 & 1992
Intern - Moore House for Runaways, Jackson, MS, 9/90 - 6/91

Note: Bernadette is not satisfied with her first job after college. She has created a resume that presents her skills in four specific areas. This resume will not "scan" into a computer with these typefaces.

Beth Hynoski
2783 STONY HILL ROAD
HARTFORD, CT 06106
203-360-9145

PROFILE   Proven ability in processing medical, disability and death claims for an
insurance carrier with a local and national client base

WORK EXPERIENCE

PRUDENTIAL INSURANCE CO., INC., Hartford, CT
Claims Processor   10/92-present
Description: Responsible for confirming eligibility of insureds and determining
appropriateness of treatment according to terms of the policy

Accomplishments:
• Processes 800 claims per month, 25% more than job criteria require
• Determines payment criteria in an average of one week, rather than
the usual average of two
• Recognized by management as an example of outstanding quality-
and-service-oriented employee

Responsibilities:
• Composes client information, eligibility and collection information on
word processor
• Obtains required information from doctors, lawyers and hospitals for
making eligibility determinations
• Processes disability and death claims

File Clerk   10/90-10/92
Description: Duties involved filing and mailing

Responsibilities:
• Opened, stamped, and sorted the mail, ensuring proper distribution.
• Filed mail and documents
• Prepared outgoing mail in a timely manner

OLSTEN TEMPORARY SERVICES, Hartford, CT   1/90-10/90
Temporary Employee
Description: Performed a variety of duties, including filing, reception, and
word processing

EDUCATION

CENTRAL CONNECTICUT STATE UNIVERSITY, Hartford, CT
Currently enrolled in liberal arts degree program

*Note: Beth is a part-time college student and a full-time employee. She includes
accomplishments and "facts and figures" in her "Work Experience."*

Carla Ramos
19842 Socorro Blvd. #2B
Odessa, TX 79763
(915) 896-3517

OBJECTIVE: A position in law enforcement, investigation, or corporate security. Offering a strong educational background, relevant experience, solid skills, and a commitment to hard work.

EDUCATION

Bachelor of Science (with Honors), May 1995
University of Texas at El Paso
Major: *Administration of Justice*
Minor: *Psychology*
Criminology Certificate
GPA: 3.68/4.0

RELEVANT COURSES:

Justice in American Society
Criminal Law
Police Organization and Administration
Sociology of Deviant Behavior
Principles of Personality

White-Collar Crime
Court Management and Administration
Juvenile Justice
Criminology
Principles of Abnormal Psychology

INTERNSHIPS

Administration of Justice, El Paso Municipal Court System, Spring 1995
■ Observation and participation in court system. Averaged 10 hours per week.

Criminology Internship, El Paso Police Department, Fall 1994
■ Worked in crime investigations unit. Responded to calls and visited crime sites with police officers. Averaged 8 hours per week.

VOLUNTEER EXPERIENCE

■ **Citizen's Advisory Committee,** Odessa Police Department, Summers, 1993 and 1994. Served as community representative and liaison with metropolitan police department. Participated in training program for CAC members. Attended more than 20 meetings with community members and police.

ACTIVITIES

Citizens Rifle and Revolver Club, Range Instructor
Junior Rifle Program (P.B.A. sponsored), Range Instructor
Target Shooting, Distinguished Expert Classification
Tang Soo Do Martial Arts

LANGUAGES

Fluent in Spanish and English (written and spoken)

Note: Notice how qualified Carla appears to be for the type of job she wants, even though she has no paid work experience.

Joseph B. Clayton

2046 Meridian Lane
Omaha, NE 68152

(402) 697-8121 work
(402) 943-0608 home

SUMMARY: More than 20 years of business experience including total responsibility for operations of companies in Europe as well as Chief Financial Officer for publicly traded company.

EXPERIENCE: T.H. James Systems, Inc., Omaha, NE   6/80-Present
Group Vice President, member of Board of Directors and
Chief Financial Officer

Responsible for all duties of Chief Financial Officer including S.E.C., Legal, E.D.P., personnel, banking, tax, shareholder relations, and other administrative duties. Operations responsibilities include management of subsidiaries in England, France, and Italy through general managers. Report to the Chief Executive Officer. Began as Treasurer. Advanced to Vice President of Finance.

Accomplishments:

- Involved in overall growth in revenues from $3,000,000 to over $50,000,000
- Orchestrated subsidiary turnaround from losing operations to successfully profitable
- Effected spin-off and initial public offering for a subsidiary
- Planned public issues of stock
- Coordinated M.I.S. systems
- Organized I.R.S. rulings for tax savings
- Negotiated lines of credit financing
- Organized building purchase, financing and additional expansion in U.S. and Europe

EDUCATION: University of Nebraska   5/72
B.S. Accounting
Certified Public Accountant License awarded   9/74

ORGANIZATIONS/ ACTIVITIES:

Delegate, Republican National Convention	1988, 1992
Member, Omaha City Council	1986-88
Chair, Financial Committee, Omaha Art Museum	1987-present
Member, Omaha Chamber of Commerce	1980-present
Member, Big Brothers of Omaha	1977-present

Note: Joe has been employed by the same firm for many years. He recounts his accomplishments effectively, using very brief statements preceded by bullets.

Emily Valdes

**8 Livingston Lane
Hackensack, NJ 07602
(201) 419-1766**

OBJECTIVE

A position in the communications industry

PERSONAL QUALIFICATIONS

- Able to express concepts clearly both orally and in writing
- Exceptional interpersonal and public relations skills
- Conscientious, meticulous, high energy self-starter who takes great pride in work
- Able to meet tight deadlines
- Solid academic experience in speech and public speaking

SKILLS

RADIO AND TELEVISION PRODUCTION
Produced community oriented television programs at MUNICIPAL CABLE STATION
- Used VHS Sony and Panasonic camera and editing equipment.
- Produced scripts for upcoming programs and special projects.

Served as newscaster and promotions assistant for WNDY RADIO STATION
- Developed scripts for newscasts which included leads and voicers.
- Established clientele to promote giveaways.

Participated in all production aspects at WKML RADIO
- Performed commercials.
- Participated in live remotes for local companies.

PUBLIC RELATIONS AND SALES
Developed a combination of effective retail selling techniques at Towne Jewelers.
- Utilized "suggestion selling" techniques, leading to effective closing and "upselling."
- Treated problem customers with patience and sensitivity, providing restitution to ensure continued patronage.

WORK HISTORY

- Student intern, City Cable Television, Hackensack, NJ, 1994
- Student intern, WKML-FM Radio, Jersey City, NJ, 1994
- Assistant store manager, Towne Jewelers, Montclair, NJ, 1990-1993

EDUCATION

B.A. Communication, Kean College, Union, NJ, 1994
A.A. Social Sciences, Bergen County Community College, Hackensack, NJ, 1992

*Note: Emily is a recent college graduate whose only paid work has been in a retail store.
Notice how she features her personal qualifications and the skills she gained
in her internships.*

Eugene Dobbs

1449-A East Point Blvd.
Decatur, GA 30034

404-642-8714 (voicemail)

PROFILE

- Over 10 years of highly successful experience with increasing responsibility in all phases of the movie exhibition industry, learning the business from the ground up
- Quick learner in converting operations from manual to automated systems
- Capable of training subordinates and peers in all phases of the theater business
- Excellent presentation, communication and interpersonal skills
- Dedicated and motivated professional with good business acumen, able to handle multifaceted tasks while meeting deadlines

CAREER

Manager, Suburban Theaters, Atlanta, GA

(1993-present)

Responsible for the entire management and operation of a multiplex theater including developing human resources; producing annual budget and financial goals; purchasing; inventory control; Information Processing implementation and maintenance; capital improvements and market development.

- Raised theater evaluation from "Not-Rated" to "Gold" within a three year period by improving physical structure and upgrading the quality and level of sound and projection equipment
- Implemented information processing system and troubleshot hardware and software
- Oversaw conversion from manual to automated ticketing system
- Established two new VIP accounts in each of the last 6 quarters, exceeding new corporate account goals
- Improved concession-per-person from $1.68 to $2.07, exceeding goals by 125% while maintaining cost goals over 3 year period
- Reduced projection booth operating costs
- Negotiated and managed contracts for capital projects, controlling costs resulting in improved operational efficiencies and reduced potential liability exposure
- Conducted market analysis of competition to create strategic marketing tactics
- Implemented a bill scanning system, reducing the threat of receiving counterfeit money

Eugene Dobbs

CAREER

Assistant Manager, Suburban Theaters, Atlanta, GA
Assistant Manager, Loews Theaters, Smyrna, GA
Projectionist, United Artists Theaters, Decatur, GA
Head Usher, General Cinema, Smyrna, GA
Usher, General Cinema, Smyrna, GA

PROFESSIONAL DEVELOPMENT

Note: All of my employers have been national theater chains and all offer professional development courses. Among the more than 15 courses I have completed are:

- Human Relations I & II
- Management by Planning
- Skills for Supervisors
- Managing People
- Increasing Productivity
- Improving Customer Service

EDUCATION

Atlanta Technical Institute, Atlanta, GA
- Introduction to Computing
- Troubleshooting PCs
- Installing Software

Stone Mountain Community College
- Psychology 101 & 102
- Introduction to Human Resources
- Retailing

AFFILIATION

- National Association of Theater Managers

Eugene began his career as a part-time usher in a local movie theater and now manages a multi-plex. Notice how he emphasizes his accomplishments and de-emphasizes dates. This is not a computer-scannable resume.

Joshua Reilly

3821 Joy Road
Detroit, MI 48206
(H) 313-405-7624 ▪ (W) 313-407-0284

OBJECTIVE

A position as Garage Supervisor with a bus transportation company

SUMMARY

Over nine years' experience in the bus transportation industry with progressive responsibility and advancement. Have served in many operational capacities, including acting Garage Manager and Depot Master.

EXPERIENCE

Michigan Transportation Authority, Detroit, MI

Regional Supervisor, Bus Operations, Wayne County, MI 11/89-present

- Mastered the knowledge of employees' contract and work requirements.
- Changed the schedules accordingly to reduce excessive overtime, and thus reduce costs.
- Handle and resolve customer complaints
- Investigate accidents, vandalism and safety hazards to reduce costs of insurance and workers' compensation
- Hear and resolve grievances before they go to arbitration
- Assist the Garage Supervisor in hiring
- Instruct over 300 new and continuing operators concerning company policy and operation

Bus Operator, Wayne County, MI 11/87-11/89

- Maintained excellent on-time record on all assigned routes
- Attained outstanding attendance record

Commercial Driver's License obtained 1/87

MILITARY SERVICE

Honorable Discharge, U.S. Air Force
Served in Vietnam
Member of Vietnam Veterans of America

Personal and Professional references available on request.

Note: In these competitive times, more and more occupations require resumes. Here is a fine example, in a field that used to require only a handwritten job application form.

Leon Jones

33 Flynn Street
Somerville, MA 02144
Home (617) 994-9927
Work (617) 309-8400 ext 349

PROFILE

▼ Over five years experience in design and development of Electro-Mechanical equipment utilizing AutoCad

▼ Accomplished in the development of new and improved products

▼ Capable of designing efficient and effective systems to improve productivity and reduce costs

▼ Work well with co-workers and external customers to establish and maintain customer satisfaction

EXPERIENCE

SPECIALIST TRANSFORMERS, INC., Cambridge, MA 1993 to Present

Mechanical Engineer

▼ Designs custom enclosures for high voltage, high current AC/DC power supplies, test equipment, switches and controls

▼ Conducts research and continual reviews of raw materials, reducing production costs

▼ Performs extensive sheetmetal layout and PC board design

▼ Inspects product during production and assembly, ensuring compliance to quality specifications

▼ Travels to sites in North America and conducts surveys to determine the needs of the customer and designs products to meet their needs within their cost estimations

▼ Works and supports sales to develop actual manufacturing costs to maintain profit margins

MASSACHUSETTS TRANSPORTATION AGENCY, Boston, MA 1991 to 1993

Engineering Assistant, part-time and summers

▼ Gathered field survey data for various highway related research projects in collaboration with project managers

▼ Wrote reports and made presentations to management

COMPUTER EXPERIENCE

Hardware	PC Platform, MacIntosh and Mini computer environment - AS-400
Applications	AutoCad rel. 12 (use and customization), Lotus 1-2-3, Microsoft Word for Windows, Claris Works, Auto-EDMS
Operating Systems	MS-DOS, Novell Networks, Windows

EDUCATION

University of Massachusetts, Boston

Bachelor of Science Degree in Industrial Engineering
1992 (3.4 GPA)

Note: The "Profile" section skillfully weaves together skills, accomplishments, and personal qualifications. For electronic scanning, the attraction-getting "bullets" should be removed.

Lilya Nasser, M.D.
124 Alder Place
Silver Spring, MD 20906
(301) 783-1219 (Home)
(301) 899-1910 (Ans. Service)

GOAL   Partnership or staff position with HMO, multi-specialty Group Practice, or hospital-affiliated Group Practice

EXPERIENCE

Physician
Staff physician with Associated Medical Arts, College Park, MD
■ Patient care in busy family medicine practice.
■ Treat common medical disorders including hypertension, bronchitis, asthma, diabetes.
■ Practice preventive medicine by screening for breast cancer, performing annual Pap smears, physical exams, etc.
■ Working in an ambulatory setting allows me to provide information and support for patients needing to modify their diets and lifestyles to prevent and reduce risks for hereditary and acquired disorders.
(1995-present)

Emergency Room Physician
Full-time position in E.R. of Capitol Hill Hospital, Washington, DC
■ Performed initial patient screening and diagnosis.
■ Handled acute emergencies including myocardial infarction, seizures, strokes, cardiac arrhythmia and meningitis on an emergency basis.
■ Triaged acute trauma victims and provided initial resuscitation and stabilization measures prior to transferring patients to a tertiary center.
■ Diagnosed and evaluated common injuries including sprains, fractures, etc. and provided initial treatment measures.
■ Diagnosed and treated common illnesses including gastroenteritis, asthma, pneumonia, and enteric fever.
■ Worked as team leader in ACLS protocol in ICU and general floors in addition to providing resuscitation measures in the emergency room.
(1994-95)

PROFESSIONAL TRAINING

Residency and internship in Internal Medicine at George Washington University Medical Center, Washington, DC (1990-94)
Third Year Resident
■ Worked as Team Leader on general Internal medicine floors.
■ Made diagnostic and therapeutic decisions about patient care and treatment.
■ Provided consultation as internist for OB/GYN and Psychiatric patients.
■ As Senior Resident and Team Leader, responsible for running the code.
■ Completed Intensive Care and Coronary Care Unit rotations, including cardiology, ventilator management, arterial blood gases and Swan-Ganz interpretations.
■ Evaluated patients in Ambulatory Clinics throughout the community.

Second Year Resident
▮ Supervised junior interns on general medicine floor, determining treatment plans and long-term care of hospitalized patients.
▮ Completed rotations in Coronary Care and Intensive Care units. Worked together with Cardiologists and Pulmonologists in care of critically ill patients with septic shock, acute respiratory failure, acute renal failure, complicated and uncomplicated myocardial infarction, and emergency hemodialysis.
▮ Performed invasive procedures including lumbar punctures, thoracentesis, endotracheal intubations, central venous catheters and Swan-Ganz.
▮ Evaluated patients in community-based Ambulatory Clinics.

First Year Resident
▮ Treated hospitalized patients with a variety of medical conditions, including complications of diabetes, pneumonia, uncontrolled hypertension, cellulitis, exacerbation of COPD, etc.
▮ Responsible to admit patients, identify problems and create a management/treatment plan under the supervision of a Senior Resident and Attending Physician.
▮ Completed several clinical rotations, including Cardiac Step-Down Unit, General Internal Medicine, Respiratory, Neurology and Oncology.
▮ Worked under Emergency Room doctor's supervision, with exposure to a broad range of emergency patients, including Pediatric, Surgical and OB/GYN.

EDUCATION

Post-Doctorate Study: George Washington University, Biological Sciences (1993-94)
M.D., University of Cairo, Cairo, Egypt (1989-93)
B.S., Biological Sciences, Cairo College for Women, Cairo, Egypt (1985-89)

AWARDS

▮ Dean's List (every semester in college and medical school), 1985-93
▮ Class Scholar (one of 3 in medical school class), 1993
▮ Outstanding Resident Award (voted by teaching faculty), 1994

PROFESSIONAL EXAMINATIONS

▮ Board Certified - Internal Medicine
▮ Foreign Medical Graduate Examination in Medical Sciences (FMGEMS), Basic Science Component - Passed 1993
▮ Foreign Medical Graduate Examination in Medical Sciences (FMGEMS), Clinical Science Component - Passed 1994

CERTIFICATIONS:

Ambulatory Care Rotation for the Community Outreach Program
Advanced Cardiac Life Support
Advanced Trauma Life Support Certificate

MEMBERSHIPS/ASSOCIATIONS:

American Medical Association
American College of Physicians

Note: Lilya has been in medical practice only a short time, so she highlights her extensive training and education.

Marvin Hulick

c/o Eldon Hulick
595 Lafin Street
St. Louis, MO 63122
(314) 706-1267

JOB OBJECTIVE: **Emergency Medical Technician or Firefighter**

CAPABILITIES

✓ Communicates swiftly and efficiently with 911 Dispatch, Police and Fire authorities in emergency situations.
✓ Exercises good judgment and leadership in crisis situations.
✓ Capably performs all types of basic life support.
✓ Provides excellent physical and emotional care for patients.
✓ Maintains a clean, well-equipped ambulance, ready for any emergency.

ACCOMPLISHMENTS

✓ Completed Squad Driving Course and maintains an excellent personal driving record.
✓ Achieved consistently high save ratios (42%) on First Aid Crew in Greene County.
✓ Worked on first aid crew granted "most reliable status" above all crews in Greene County.
✓ Awarded "Best Appearing Ambulance," Springfield Memorial Day Parade

CERTIFICATIONS & TRAINING

✓ EMT-A, 120 Hours
✓ CPR, American Red Cross, on-going
✓ HAZ-MAT, Awareness Certification, 16 Hours
✓ Heavy Vehicle Extraction, 8 Hours
✓ Confined Space Training, 16 Hours

EXPERIENCE

EMERGENCY MEDICAL TECHNICIAN
Davis Ambulance Service
EMERGENCY MEDICAL TECHNICIAN
Greene County First Aid & Rescue Squad
FIREFIGHTER
Bolivar Fire Company

EDUCATION

Graduated Walton High School, Bolivar, MO

Plan to enroll in Associate Degree Program for Fire Science, Frontenac Community College

Note: All of Marvin's experience came as an unpaid volunteer, but he treats volunteer work as if it were paid work. This resume is not likely to be electronically scanned, but it will not scan cleanly without removing the checkmarks.

Moses Johnson

919 Third Avenue
Greensboro, NC 27405
(910) 497-3712

PROFILE
12 years of experience in Heavy Construction industry. 10 years in utilities construction. Present position: General Foreman

EMPLOYMENT
General Foreman, Piedmont Construction Co., Greensboro, NC 1991-present
Responsible for the supervision of all phases of the placement and installation of gas, electric and telephone distribution work.
- ✦ Responsible for installation of utilities using the Horizontal Directional Boring Method
- ✦ Communicate effectively the goals and objectives of each project and work with the assigned crew to complete work on time and within the established quality standards
- ✦ Implement knowledge of OSHA as a company Certified OSHA Compliance Supervisor to ensure job safety, reducing lost work time and insurance premiums
- ✦ Coach subordinates in the best methods and proper use of tools to improve productivity
- ✦ Work with company management and contractor's inspectors and engineers on daily basis to ensure quality of completed project
- ✦ Plan the most effective and efficient operations to complete projects and order required materials
- ✦ Perform repaving and landscape restoration to close out project

Heavy Construction Laborer, Piedmont Construction Co., Greensboro, NC 1987-91
- ✦ Performed as a member of a work crew all phases of gas, telephone and electric utility work

Heavy Construction Laborer, Local 734, Greensboro, NC 1984-87
- ✦ Assigned to various heavy construction projects including road construction, landscaping, concrete and a long term assignment on the construction of a sewage treatment plant

EDUCATION/TRAINING
Certification in Construction Management,
Greater Greensboro Community College, 1992

OSHA Compliance Training, 1993

Safety and Education Certification, Heavy Construction Laborer Local 734, 1991

PERSONAL
Member and elder, AME Zion Church, Greensboro, NC

Note: Moses has progressed from laborer to a general foreman and has gone back to school as well. His resume describes this progression nicely. Moses does not work in an occupation in which electronic scanning of resumes is common.

Raymond Thieu
168 Chesterfield Road
Richmond, VA 23221
(804) 799-5355

BIOLOGICAL SCIENCES/ANIMAL BEHAVIOR

SUMMARY

A recent college graduate with a solid education in biology and strong background in animal care and management.

QUALIFICATIONS

- Enthusiastic, diligent worker
- Excellent laboratory skills
- Able to take direction well
- Work effectively as a team member
- Quick learner

EDUCATION

B.S., Biology, University of Virginia, June 1994
    Emphasis: Zoology
    GPA in major: 3.6 (on 4.0 scale)
Relevant Courses

Mammology	Microbiology
Zoology	Organic Chemistry
Physiology (Vertebrates)	Animal Behavior
Genetics	Ecology

EMPLOYMENT

Department Manager: Mammals
Super Pet, Richmond, VA, 6/94-Present
- Supervise and direct the activities of departmental staff.
- Interview and hire all personnel.
- Order all products sold in the department.

Pet Groomer, Super Pet, 6/93-6/94
- Full-time summer job and weekend job during school year
- Responsible for grooming all animals by appointment
- Groomed dogs, cats, and other mammals, including ferrets, raccoons, skunks, etc.

Veterinary Assistant, Summers, 1992, 1993
- Assisted in all phases of office
- Assisted in examinations and surgery

PERSONAL

- Active member of biological sciences club, University of Virginia
- Assistant Leader, Science Explorer Post #115
- Dog handler and participant in numerous American Kennel Club sanctioned dog shows. Handler of Grand Champion Russian Wolfhound.

Note: Here is a recent college graduate who has designed an excellent resume. He has structured it so that a potential employer will want to keep reading.

Mae Li, Attorney at Law
Bay Village Park, B-208
Lakewood, OH 44107

216-474-1800 (office) 216-495-1680 (beeper) 216-489-1215 (home)

SUMMARY OF QUALIFICATIONS

Management:
- Skilled in direction of research and planning in trial and pre-trial strategy
- Maintain extensive client contact in high volume practice
- Accomplished negotiator and arbitrator
- Supervision of large clerical staff in a law office environment

Litigation:
- Extensive attainments in all phases of civil litigation
- Successfully conducted depositions and jury trials in personal injury cases
- Vast experience in the arbitration process as a party and a mediator
- Practice in all areas of Family Law including divorce, separation agreements, adoption and child custody

CAREER HISTORY

Associate, Beauchamp & Cline, Cleveland, OH
- Civil Trial Attorney
- Family Law section supervisor
  Extensive trial experience with busy urban law firm employing approximately 75 attorneys.
  (1991–present)

Associate, Cooper/Boniske, Akron, OH
- Civil Trial Attorney
- Supervisor of paraprofessional staff
  Trial and management experience in medium-sized law firm employing approximately 35 attorneys.
  (1986–91)

Law Clerk, Great Lakes Petroleum, Cleveland, OH
- Review, analysis and maintenance of oil and gas leases
- Assisted attorneys in drafting tax partnership agreements
- Initiated conferences with landowners on behalf of company
- Conducted property surveys involving oil and gas leases
  Clerkship in major regional corporation that employed 10 full-time attorneys.
  (1983–86)

EDUCATION

J.D., University of Akron, 1983
B.A., University of Ohio, 1978
Peace Corps Volunteer, Cambodia, 1978–80
Admitted to Ohio State Bar, 1983

Note: This resume is quite well organized. The "Summary of Qualifications" has two separate sections, each of interest to a prospective employer. If this resume is ever "scanned," a human "verifier" can easily remove the bullets.

Richard Jasiewicz

194 Lassen Drive
Yuba City, CA 95991
916-479-5325

COMPUTER SYSTEMS SUPERVISION/DATA COMMUNICATION

—SUMMARY PROFILE—

Offering 4 years of progressively responsible experience in computer installation and local area network management. Skilled in both technical and administrative supervision.

—EXPERIENCE—

United States Air Force
Edwards Air Force Base
Boron, CA
(1992-1996)

Secure Communications Systems Supervisor, Quality Assurance Inspector
- Responsible for the maintenance, repair, modification and installation of all cryptographic and microcomputer systems in support of the 466th Air Base Wing. Total installation exceeded 150 computers.
- Determined work procedures, estimated costs, and requisitioned needed materials. Annual budget exceeded $400,000.
- Submitted justification for manpower requirements to higher headquarters and analyzed budget requirements for each fiscal year.
- Assigned duties to subordinates; wrote personnel performance reports and provided counseling when needed. Supervised staff of 5.
- Performed equipment inspections and personnel evaluations to measure the quality and degree of maintenance and training within each facet of the unit.

Data Networks Team Evaluator, Team Safety Supervisor
- Primary duties consisted of testing Air Force communication lines worldwide to verify conformance to government regulations by ensuring that specifications were being met using test instruments such as the Hekimian 7000 analog test set, Phoenix 500 and Firebird 5000 bit error rate test sets.
- Generated reports which were forwarded to Headquarters, United States Air Force for review and action.
- Responsible for an equipment account of more than $100,000.
- Used protocol analyzers such as the Digilog 600 to evaluate data integrity and flow control.
- Executed duties as cable fabrications expert and microcomputer repair technician for all assigned computer systems.
- Special Duty Assignment requiring former Commander's endorsements and recommendations.

Richard Jasiewicz-2

Assistant Work Center Supervisor, Squadron Safety Supervisor
- Coordinated activities of up to 10 workers engaged in the installation, modification, maintenance and repair of cryptographic and teletype equipment.
- Reviewed Maintenance Data Collection documentation, supply logs and trouble reports for completeness and accuracy.
- Aggressively managed the work centers training program.
- Key person in establishing and operating the Base Small Computer Support Center, performing duties such as base computer systems inventory, setting up computer and software training classes, performing computer maintenance and repair, and trouble shooting software problems.
- Carried out base level safety duties such as building inspections and conducting spot inspections and safety meetings.

—EDUCATION & TRAINING—

Associates Degree in Electronic Systems Technology
Community College of the Air Force
Degree Awarded 1995

Courses included:
- Narrowband Subscriber Terminal Course
- Burroughs B25 E-Mail Administrator's and User's Course
- Worldwide Networks Systems Evaluation Course 8
- Organizational and Intermediate Maintenance
- HQ AFLC Training Division "C" Language Programming Course
- Logistics Systems Architects Harvard Graphics Training Program
- Information Systems Technology Center Zenith Z-248 Microcomputer Repair
- Communication Electronics Quality Control Procedures Course
- Pacific Air Forces Quality Awareness and Unit Assessment Course
- Air Mobility Command Teams and Tools Course
- USAF Effective Writing Course (AFCC NCO Leadership School)
- Air Force Supervisor's Course

—MEMBERSHIPS—

Communication Electronics Association
U.S. Air Force Reserve

—PERSONAL—

Willing and able to travel and/or relocate.

Note: All of Richard's experience and education have occurred in the Air Force.
He has done an outstanding job of describing them in "civilian" language.

Benita Rojas 985 Estes Blvd.Eugene, OR 08690 (503) 698-3768

Seeking position as a Veterinary Technician specializing in Anesthesiology.

EDUCATION
University of Oregon, Eugene, OR B.S., Biology   October, 1994

Relevant Coursework: Applied Microbiology   Animal Physiology
Vertebrate Zoology   Mammalogy
Organic Chemistry   Genetics
Horse Management   Animal Behavior

Additional Studies: Graduate level Microbiology, University of Oregon, 1995

EXPERIENCE
Veterinary Technician   1992-Present
Lane Animal Hospital, Springfield, Oregon
- Assist in small animal surgery by monitoring anesthesia, heart rate and respiratory rate.
- Manage inventory of drug and food products.
- Prepare and read microscopic tests on blood, urine and feces.
- Assist in physical examination of animals.

Laboratory Assistant   1990-1992
Steek Drug Company, Eugene, Oregon   (summers)
- Prepared and conducted laboratory test of drugs being currently developed by Steek.

Voluntary Veterinary Assistant   1990-1992
Eugene Animal Shelter, Eugene, Oregon
- Assisted vets (who were also volunteers) in medical treatment of animals in the shelter.

Veterinary Assistant   1988-1990
Azalez Animal Hospital, Azalez, Oregon   after school and summers
- Assisted vets in whatever way necessary.

EXTRA-CURRICULAR ACTIVITIES
Programs Coordinator
Veterinary Science Club, University of Oregon
- Organized field trips and speakers for VSC meetings.

INTERESTS/PERSONAL
- Fundraiser and volunteer for local small animal shelter.
  Raised $10,000 last year for shelter.
- Coordinator of area Neuter/Spay Awareness Program.

Note: Benita is a recent college graduate with very little paid experience, but she has blended her education and unpaid experience into an outstanding resume.

Elyse Mangiotti
1449 Concord Place #4
Boston, MA 02128

617-942-7658 (office)
617-942-7659 (fax)
617-846-5112 (home)

SUMMARY OF QUALIFICATIONS

Experienced sales and marketing professional with a record of consistent accomplishment in pioneering and building profitable territories, exceeding planned revenue production and cost control goals, capturing and managing key accounts, developing and implementing strategic plans to penetrate uncharted markets.

Motivated self-starter with strong organizational, decision-making, communication and problem-solving skills.

SELECTED ACCOMPLISHMENTS
Sales

- Pioneered new territory, increasing sales from zero to $1+ million in 1+ years.
- Surpassed revenue targets by 140% of quota.
- Reversed declining territory sales by reviving dormant accounts, increasing customer base and capturing new accounts.
- Increased territory sales an average of 12% which contributed to substantial revenue, cash flow and profit increases.
- Managed 200+ accounts concurrently, consistently growing sales and maintaining long term profitable relationships.
- Forecasted and managed budgets, consistently achieving goals for revenue production and cost control.
- Recruited, trained, motivated and built cohesive field sales team that consistently exceeded sales and sales-to-expense goals.

Marketing

- Directed the profitable re-launch of exclusive Salon Stylistics line, including logistics planning and timing of inventory shipments to distributors.
- Coordinated planning, implementation and activities of trade shows, conventions and presentations throughout the USA. Heightened product visibility and generated substantial new sales.
- Developed highly profitable market plan, for an open product line, which was sold to salons through a multi-state distributor network.
- Researched, formulated and managed programs, with focus on drug stores and beauty salons, which resulted in deep penetration of target market segments.

PROFESSIONAL EXPERIENCE

National Sales Manager, Salon Systematics, Boston MA, 1994–present

District Sales Manager, BonaVitae, Fort Lee, NJ, 1992–94

Regional Sales Manager, Biltrite Office Furniture, Philadelphia, PA, 1989–92

Sales Representative (Commercial Accounts), Freedom Furniture,
Cherry Hill, NJ, 1988–89

Available to travel and relocate

Note: Elyse put a lot of effort into this resume and it shows! See how she phrases her accomplishments and how well she includes "facts and figures." This entire resume is in an italic typeface. Elyse will need to reformat it for electronic scanning.

CONFIDENTIAL RESUME
Carmen Quentin
Capitol Building
Room 1440
Nashville, TN 37203
615-530-1199

Profile:

Experienced administrator who currently manages the office of the Governor of Tennessee. Especially skilled at planning and supervising complex projects.

Strengths:

- Proficient in management of busy organizations with high diversity of responsibilities, needs and constituencies.
- Excellent speech writer and presenter; official representative at meetings with a wide variety of groups.
- Extensive marketing/public relations experience in both government and industry.
- Adept at troubleshooting and problem-solving.
- Skilled supervisor, able to manage both scheduling and staffing responsibilities.

Experience:

Director of Staff, Governor's Office, Nashville, TN (1992–present)
- Oversee all functions of a busy office.
- Supervise staff of five in scheduling travel arrangements, meetings, public forums, speeches, presentations and appearances by the Governor, his staff and the first Lady.
- Represent the Governor at his meetings of municipal government representatives, mayors, special constituent groups and citizens.
- Draft speeches and official correspondence for the Governor.

Marketing Director, Shapiro/Levin Attorneys at Law, Memphis, TN (1989–1992)
- Developed strategic marketing plan for firm with 19 attorneys.
- Organized both external and internal promotional and public relations activities for the firm.

- Represented the firm to the community at corporate, social and political events.
- Composed press releases, promotional materials and presentations.
- Designed presentation materials and mailings.

General Manager, Capitol City Printing, Nashville, TN (1990–92)
- Supervised office and office staff for high-volume printing company with annual sales volume of more than $2,000,000.
- Implemented new computerized office system that speeded billing and reduced costs.
- Created diversified marketing plan, including newspaper, direct mail, and specialty ad placements.
- Responsible for all office operations, including administration, bookkeeping, personnel and scheduling.

Additional Experience:
- **Executive Director**, Realtors Association of Greater Memphis
- **Assistant Director**, American Red Cross Regional Office, Memphis, TN
- **Office Manager**, Legal Aid Society of Nashville
- **Assistant to the Director**, Tennessee State AFL-CIO, Nashville, TN

Volunteer Experience:
Coordinator, Governor's Literacy Campaign fund-raiser
- Supervised all aspects of events that raised more than $1,000,000 for literacy education.

Director, "Raise the Roof"
- Oversaw entire campaign that raised more than $750,000 for Habitat for Humanity.

Assistant Coordinator, "Blood for Life"
- Assisted in managing emergency blood drive that attracted more than 8,000 new donors.

Education:
Attended Tennessee State University. Major: Business Administration

NOTE: PLEASE RESPECT THE CONFIDENTIALITY OF THIS RESUME

Note: Carmen has a variety of skills and has held a number of jobs. See how he describes himself first, then his paid work, and finally his volunteer work. Observe, too, how he requests confidentiality.

Clarence E. Lee

221 Bensen Ave.
Harwood Heights, IL 60656
(312) 901-9147 (Home)
(312) 250-3349 (Work)
(312) 717-1868 (Cellular)

OBJECTIVE: Seasoned, highly experienced management executive with extensive supervisory and personnel expertise seeks new challenges and opportunities in a firm with the potential for increased sales/profits.

EXPERIENCE: Village Market, Inc. (1985–present)

Senior Supervisor (1994–present)
- Supervise 24 retail convenience stores in Northern and Western Chicago area with annual gross sales of $32 million.
- Train managers, assistant managers and employees in all aspects of retail operations, including supervision, purchasing, inventory, scheduling, cash management, problem resolution, and profitability enhancement.
- Participate in budget preparation for each store and monitor targets to ensure goals are achieved.
- Inspect stores regularly to ascertain compliance with company policies and standards.
- Coordinate with Human Resource Manager in the recruiting, hiring and training of store personnel and ongoing development of the management team.
- Work closely with the Area Marketing Manager in the implementation of promotional programs, remodels and new stores.
- Co-author of extensive step-by-step training manual for store personnel.

District Supervisor (1989–94)
- Directed operations of 12 stores.

Store Manager, Northern Illinois region (1986–89)
- Opened 30 new locations; specialized in advancing new operations and establishing positive image/impact in neighborhoods.

EDUCATION:

Edutech of Chicago, Schiller Park, IL
- Extensive, hands-on, personalized computer training via courses in Windows, Project Management, Graphics, Spreadsheets and Database Management.

Clarence E. Lee
Page 2

EDUCATION:

Elmhurst College, Elmhurst, IL
- National Restaurant Association Applied Food Service Sanitation Course; earned Certification in Sanitation and Food Handling.

Belmont University, Chicago, IL
- Food Management and Marketing

Dale Carnegie, Chicago, IL
- Effective Speaking & Human Relations

ORGANIZATIONS:

Member, Greater Chicago Chamber of Commerce
Member, Illinois Food Council
Member, Greater Chicago Food Council

**CHARITABLE
ACTIVITIES: Arden Institute for Autism**

- Advisory Panel for employment of the handicapped.
- 10–year fundraising and organizational volunteer.
- Raised in excess of $500,000 for the Institute.
- Assisted in fundraising for construction of Village House for diagnosis and treatment of autism in infants and children to age 5.
- Established Village Care Mobile Unit to bring diagnostic and treatment services for autism to the community.
- Helped initiate Village Camp for autistic children and families.

Children's Miracle Network
- Aid in special events and fundraising for nationwide network assisting children and their families with serious illnesses.

Mission House
- Assist in organization of annual Christmas party for over 1,200 Mission House children at the MacCormick Convention Center.

*Note: Here is an excellent way to handle experience with only one employer.
The "Charitable Activities" demonstrate strong commitment to the community.*

Darlene T. McMahon
26938 Winterdown Court, Tustin, California 92681
714-360-0682

Recreation and Resort Management

Qualifications:
– Excellent training in recreation theory and practice
– Experience at one of the nation's most prestigious theme parks
– Energetic, dedicated, gregarious, hard-working

Education:
Bachelor of Science, Recreation 1994
California State University at Fullerton
Minor: Business Management

Experience:

Trainer/Human Resources, Disneyland, Anaheim, CA 2/95–present
– Interviewed, evaluated, hired and processed employees for full
and part-time jobs; staff exceeded 5000 at peak season. An average
of 70,000 guests visit the park every day at peak season.
– Oriented and trained new and returning staff at the "University of
Disneyland," the Park's training center. Topics covered included
proper clothing, grooming, and interactions with guests.
– Trained staff in "Crime Stoppers" program against counterfeit
currency, shoplifting and internal theft.
– Educated staff on "Right to Know" laws.
– Recruited potential staff at off-site locations.
– Conducted tours of the facility, scheduled training, resolved problems,
coordinated volunteers.
– Expedited all employee-related paperwork and forms.
– Coordinated "Fun Olympics" to build staff loyalty/friendships.

Recreation Director, Hotel de la Mirada Resort and Country Club, 7/94–1/95
– Hired, trained, evaluated and scheduled recreational staff of nearly 100.
– Supervised pool, health club and tennis courts.
– Developed activities for Kids' Camp and weekend programs.
– Consulted and worked closely with resort staff in planning events.
– Edited and published Country Club Newsletter.

Recreation and Resort Management

Experience:
(continued)

– Reorganized/updated membership listings utilizing Macintosh computer.
– Organized and implemented highly successful "Safe Halloween Extravaganza."

Professional Experiences:

– Member, Resort and Commercial Recreation Association
– Volunteer Recreation Assistant, Hidden Valley Resort, 1993 and 1994
– Hostess Coordinator, Top Notch Steak House, 1990 and 1991
– Certified US Water Fitness and Water Safety Instructor
– Certified in CPR and First Aid
– Skilled in use of Macintosh and PC computers
– Traveled extensively in Europe and North America

Awards/Honors:

Cal State Fullerton University: Chairman of the Year Award, Recreation Dept.; Vice President, Recreation Club; Peer Educator: Alcohol Awareness Program

References:

Available from Placement Office, California State University at Fullerton, Fullerton, CA 92884

Note: Darlene has been employed only a brief time, but she highlights her experience well. The blend of "Professional Experiences" should catch an employer's attention.

DARLENE STRONGHEART   14 Tall Tree Court
Mobridge, SD 57601   (605) 683-7605

Certified Radiologic Technologist relocating to Denver, Colorado, summer 1996. Seeking position in office, hospital, HMO, clinic, or other health care provider.

EDUCATION/CERTIFICATION

Diploma
School of Radiological Technology
Black Hills Medical Center,
Rapid City, South Dakota

Certification in Mammography
American Registry of Radiologic
Technologists

Licensure
Radiologic Technologist,
State of South Dakota

Association
American Society of Radiologic
Technologists

Certification in Radiography
American Registry of Radiologic
Technologists

Certification
BCLS, American Heart Association

EXPERIENCE
Radiologic Technologist
Little Eagle Health Center, Mobridge, South Dakota
- Complete responsibility for departmental operations.
- Maintain files for State inspection.
- Establish and maintain complete Quality Assurance program for the department.
- Experienced in use of Picker Clinic 500 high-frequency equipment and Medix computer system.
- Schedule technologists for the department.
- Troubleshoot equipment problems and maintain service and preventative maintenance records on all x-ray equipment.
- Clean and maintain cassettes and x-ray equipment as well as Kodak X-omatic processors.

DARLENE STRONGHEART
Page 2

Mammographer/Radiologic Technologist
Mobridge Community Hospital, Mobridge, South Dakota
- Perform diagnostic radiographic procedures on out-patient basis, including Mammography, Fluoroscopy and General Radiography.
- Assist Radiologist in patient care.
- Perform and maintain all aspects of Quality assurance for ACR requirements in Mammography.

Unit Secretary - Orthopedic/Medical/Surgical Unit
Mobridge Community Hospital, Mobridge, South Dakota
- Transcribed all in-patient doctors' orders, including medications, physical therapy, dietary, nursing, scheduling of inpatient examinations and laboratory studies.
- Extensive intra-unit and inter-department communications.
- Posted laboratory and examination reports on in-patient charts.
- Performed above duties on all units of hospital, including ICU, ER, OR, CCU, Pediatrics, Oncology, Neurology, Psychiatry.

PERSONAL PROFILE
Native American raised on Standing Rock Indian Reservation in northern South Dakota. Mobridge is the only major city in the region. Little Eagle Health Center serves mostly tribal members and low-income families in Mobridge. Mobridge Community Hospital is the only hospital for more than 100 miles in any direction and serves as a hospital for dozens of small towns. My husband has accepted a job in Denver and we anticipate moving in the near future.

Note: Darlene comes to life in this nicely personalized resume. She is forthcoming about her relocation and straightforward about her experience.

EDWARD N. HIGHWATER, JR.

39 Rock River Road
Farthing, Wyoming 82054
(307) 309-2940

OBJECTIVE: Seeking responsible position in Corrections Administration/ Supervision.Offering more than 30 years of experience in corrections supervision and development.

STRENGTHS:

- Corrections program evaluation, implementation, development and revisions, including Food Service, Social Services, Medical, Maintenance, Recreation, Personnel and Training, Work Programs, Mail and Visit programs, and Inmate Work Release.

- Custody supervision experience, including Housing Unit supervision, Minimum Custody supervision, separation of inmates by crime and/or behavior.

- Implemented development programs for more than 500 inmates at a time.

- All phases of the administrative structure of the County Jail, including development of policies and procedures, their implementation and revision.

- Liaison between the State Department of Corrections and County Jails.

- Implementation of successful disciplinary programs and staff education on disciplinary issues.

- Classifications of inmates at all custody levels.

- Design and construction for renovations, additions and new construction.

- Staff hiring, development and training. Ran 10 staff development programs per year.

- Staff analysis and evaluation. Evaluated 50 officers per year at Wyoming State Prison.

- Inspection of facilities to assure compliance with all applicable federal, state and local standards.

- Completion of all required reports and documentation.

- Technical advisor to State Attorney General on county jails and municipal lock-ups.

- Representative of the Department of Corrections at public meetings and planning boards to define and clarify policies and standards promulgated by the Department.

EXPERIENCE: **STATE OF WYOMING, DEPARTMENT OF CORRECTIONS**
(1965–present)
Supervising Program Development Specialist
(1/89–present)
Program Development Specialist
(8/86–1/89)
Program Assistant
(9/84–8/86)
Senior Inspector
(11/81–9/84)
Correction Sergeant
(6/78–11/81)
Senior Correction Officer and Correction Officer
(11/65–6/78)

EDUCATION: B.S., Criminal Justice & Psychology, 1980
Laramie State College, Laramie, Wyoming

PROFESSIONAL ORGANIZATIONS:
Member, American Correctional Association
Member, American Jail Association
Member, Wyoming Warden Association

PERSONAL: *Leader, Eagle Scout Troop 147*
Co-Chair, United Way Membership Campaign for Laramie County, 1995
Willing to relocate.

Note: Ed has worked his way up a career ladder and he is ready to move on. He devotes the resume to his "Strengths" (which are actually experiences and accomplishments) and creates a compelling resume.

Susanna N. Peddie

816 Hampton Ave.
Swanzey, NH 03431
(603) 709-5849

OBJECTIVE: Seeking a position in Customer Service which utilizes extensive experience and success in satisfying clients.

STRENGTHS:
- Supervisory experience in Customer Relations.
- Skilled at problem resolution in a fast-paced environment.
- Excellent interpersonal communication skills; excel in assuring that customer needs are met and satisfactory answers to problems and questions are provided.
- Developed computerized complaint tracking and reporting system currently in use by Monadnock Customer Service Unit.
- Excellent computer skills including IBM, Macintosh, Windows, Excel and Microsoft Works.

EXPERIENCE: *Customer Service Liaison/Complaint Coordinator*
Monadnock Bank, NA, Keene, NH   1988–1995
- Directly responsible for resolving all customer service complaints and problems for the entire Central Customer Service Unit.
- Produced monthly reports tracking complaint data.
- Tracked Customer Service Representative complaint handling successes/failures and produced monthly report to Management.
- Coordinated efficiency reports between Customer Service Reps and Management, and provided recommendations for overall CSR complaint-handling improvements.
- Began as CSR: advanced to Customer Service Liaison.

Customer Relations Supervisor, Loan Division
Shawmut Bank, Manchester, NH   1986–1988

AWARDS:
- Employee of the Month: 1989, 1990, 1992
- Customer Service Award for most complimentary letters, 1993
- Monadnock Bank Award for exceptional customer service; 1994

SEMINARS:
- Mediation and Arbitration in Customer Disputes
- Win-Win Negotiation
- The Role of Customer Relations in Sales

PERSONAL: Sell handspun and dyed yarn from home-based business, "Wee Willie Yarns".

Note: Susanna has done a terrific job of integrating skills, experiences, accomplishments and personal qualifications. There is no "Education" section (intentionally) but it isn't really needed.

EVELYN NIERDORF
182 Chestnut Street, Minot, ND 58704
(701) 876-1243 (voice mail)

SUMMARY
✓ Experienced secondary school adminstrator with strong teaching and coaching background.
✓ Excellent supervisor and motivator.
✓ Effective disciplinarian.
✓ Capable liaison among departments and between teachers and principal

PROFESSIONAL EXPERIENCE
Vice Principal, Minot Regional High School   (1991–present)
- Supervisor of curriculum and Professional Development for public high school with students and 72 teachers.
- Responsible for quality and content of all classroom instruction.
- Coordinate all professional development and in-service training. Personally conduct at least 10 training sessions each school year.
- Evaluate all teachers annually.
- Oversee activities of Instructional Improvement Team.
- Coordinate home instruction programs.
- Monitor special education program.
- Assure curriculum compliance with district and state guidelines.
- Manage parent-teacher program. Coordinate back-to-school night in fall and teacher appreciation day in spring.

Teacher, English and Humanities   (1984–91)
  Minot Regional High School
Athletic Director   (1984–91)
  Minot Regional High School
Teacher, English   (1980–84)
  Robards Middle School, Bismarck, ND
Tennis Coach, Varsity/Jr. Varsity Women   (1980–84)
  Robards Middle School

EDUCATION
M.A. School Administration and Supervision   B.A. English
  Minot State University, 1990   Dickinson State University
Supervisor and Principal Certificate, 1990   Secondary Teaching Certificate, 1980

PERSONAL EXPERIENCE
Volunteer Teacher, "Project Bootstrap," Minot, ND
(supplemental education for underprivileged children).

Note: Evelyn includes an attention-getting "Summary" and then describes in detail only her present job. If she applies for a new job and knows that her resume will be "scanned," she will have to simplify its appearance.

Paul K. Nelson
712 Camino Seco Rd #92
Tucson, Arizona 85710
(602) 309-2503

CAREER OBJECTIVE: A position as a Golf Professional, where experience, proven skills and communication abilities will contribute to the success of the club.

PROFESSIONAL QUALIFICATIONS:

- PGA Member
- Completed PGA Business School I and II
- Attended various PGA seminars, including *The Art of Teaching*

EXPERIENCE:

Doredo Golf Club, Tucson, Arizona   6/94–Present
First Assistant Golf Professional

- Assistant Professional at public club accommodating approximately 55,000 rounds annually.
- Responsible for golf shop, tournament operations and outings.
- Handle computerized operations of handicaps, inventory and book-keeping.
- Schedule and teach lessons, manage sales, golf-club fitting and repairs.
- Accountable for financial operations, closing out cash register, dropping off bank deposits.
- Manage marketing, including merchandising and promotions.
- Oversee purchasing and ordering, golf cart management and rulings.

Highlight:

- Coordinate and teach summer junior golf program and women's golf classes.
- Wrote a pamphlet, *The Little Blue Book,* to promote the Golf Club.

Rolling Hills Golf Club, Tucson, Arizona   6/93–6/94
Assistant Golf Professional

- Golf Professional at private club with 300 members.
- Responsible for teaching and playing golf with members, and for tournament operations (organizing events, marking the course and scoring).
- Maintained golf carts, bag room and driving range; performed club repairs.
- Handled merchandising, promotions and computerized handicap records.
- Supervised golf shop operations, procedures and policies.

Paul K. Nelson

Highlight:
- Organized charity benefit golf tournament, "Birdie for the Childre", which raised nearly $10,000 for local children's charities.

Wildcreek Golf & Country Club, Reno, Nevada
Assistant Golf Professional   6/92–6/93
- Golf Professional at semi-private club with 150 members.
- Responsibilities included overseeing the golf shop (total coverage), memberships, golf cart operations, course rangers, starters, range boys, outings, teaching and representing the Club in tournaments.
- Handled handicapping with manual system.

Highlight:
- Substitute Golf Instructor for University of Nevada at Reno.

Nevada Bob's Discount Golf, Reno, Nevada
Manager   1/91–6/92
- Responsible for Customer Service, scheduling, employee supervision and training, departmental paper work.
- Managed inventory and security procedures.
- Consistently excelled in sales of golf equipment, with many referrals.

Played Western States PGA Mini-Tour   1/90–1/91

STRENGTHS:
- Expertise in communication and interacting with people.
- Proven self-starter with excellent motivation and self-discipline.
- Team player with effective and efficient organizational and time management skills.
- Ability to assess and prioritize needs, follow through on assignments, and function well under deadline restraints.

EDUCATION:
University of Nevada at Las Vegas
Major: Business Administration

ACHIEVEMENTS:
- Member of four-year traveling university men's golf team. During this period, ranked #1 in league several times.
- 1987, 1988 and 1991 Long Distance Driving Champion of Western States Division.
- Finished in top 10 in 1988 Nevada State Amateur.
- Two-time winner of Men's Club Championship at Desert Inn Golf Club, Las Vegas.

Interested in relocating.

Note: The challenge that Paul meets in his resume is to take his everyday routine tasks and phrase them as "experience." Adding a "highlight" allows him to communicate his selected accomplishments.

MAY HONG, MSW, ACSW
3825 Preston Road
Seattle, WA
(206) 884-8849

OBJECTIVE: Professional Social Work position in an institutional or school setting.

SKILLS SUMMARY

- Provide direct clinical services and community referrals.
- Initiate, plan and present educational seminars.
- Perform public speaking functions and serve as community liaison.
- Negotiate with government agencies, volunteer groups and consumers.

PERSONAL QUALIFICATIONS:

- Patient
- Calm, clear-thinking in crisis situations
- Excellent listener and negotiator
- Effective communicator in a variety of contexts

PROFESSIONAL EXPERIENCE:

Private Practice   1989-present

- Provide individual, family and marital therapy to a broad-based clinical population.
- Specialize in short-term treatment for adolescents and adults with substance abuse problems.

Director of Social Services   1985-1989
Seattle Hospital, Seattle, WA

- Formulated and directed clinical activites and policies for the social services department, especially counseling and discharge planning for medical patients.
- Primarily responsible for supervising and evaluating clerical staff and reviewing treatment plans.
- Administered direct service programs to high-risk areas of hospital (ER, Post-Partum, MICU, and SICU).
- Provided staff and programs for Personnel office and Employee Health service for on-site mental health problems.

Treatment Team Leader
1982-1985
Tacoma Psychiatric Center, Tacoma, WA
- Coordinated treatment services for Geriatric Admissions Unit.
- Supervised 35 clinical service employees, reviewing their treatment plans and procedures.
- Administered 7 day/24 hour crisis intervention service.
- Served as liaison and resource with communities.

Social Worker   1981-1982
San Francisco State University Medical Center Home Care Program, San Francisco, CA
- Provided direct clinical services to homebound cancer patients.
- Served on the University Home Care Advisory Board

EDUCATION:
- Master of Social Work   1981
  California State University at San Francisco
- Bachelor of Science, Speech Pathology/Audiology 1978
  California State University at San Francisco

LICENSURE/CERTIFICATION:
- Application currently pending for School Social Work license-Eligibility confirmed.
- Certified Social Worker in Washington State (CSW)
- Licensure in Washington for reimbursement
- Academy of Certified Social Workers (ACSW)
- California and Washington State Certified Teacher of the Speech and Hearing Impaired (Permanent Certification)

PROFESSIONAL AFFILIATIONS:
- National Association of Social Workers, Washington Chapter

PUBLICATIONS/SPEAKING ENGAGEMENTS/CONSULTATIONS:
- "Community Resources for Cancer Patients and their Families"
- "Handbook of Everyday Living Problems"
- Visiting Lecturer, University of Washington (Seattle) Medical School: "Mental Health Needs and Home Care Services"
- Visiting Lecturer, University of Washington (Seattle) Medical School: "The Geriatic Patient and Long Term Care Services"

References will be furnished upon request.

Note: This resume demonstrates how effective it is to include summaries of skills and personal qualifications. It is also extremely well organized.

FRANK NIVEO 1610 Mariana Way, #16B Mesa, AZ 85208

(602) 259-1328 (office) (602) 361-1440 (cellular)

Offering extensive experience in Corporate Commercial Real Estate. Substantial knowledge of all aspects of corporate leasing and development. Skilled negotiator.

EXPERIENCE

Winchell's Donuts, Regional Development Office   (1992–present)
Scottsdale, AZ

Real Estate Manager

- ❑ Responsible for all site selection for major franchise operation in Arizona and New Mexico—approximately 24 new sites per year.
- ❑ Responsible for all lease negotiations.
- ❑ Responsible for all approvals including city, country, and state.
- ❑ Responsible for coordination between architects, contractors, attorneys, engineers and traffic consultants.
- ❑ Responsible for distribution and execution of legal documents including Franchise Agreement, Development Agreement,Cross Guarantee, Corporate Resolution, Lease Option Agreement, and Federal Disclosure Certificates.
- ❑ Responsible for creation of exclusive territories for franchise owners along with the development schedules for those territories.

Suncoast Properties   (1989–92)
Costa Mesa, CA

Director of Real Estate

- ❑ Responsible for leasing of all properties.
- ❑ Oversaw site selection for shopping centers in Los Angeles and Orange Counties.
- ❑ Obtained all approvals from municipalities and state.
- ❑ Liaison between architects and engineers for shopping center design and construction.
- ❑ Coordinated all real estate and leasing for expansion of South Coast Plaza, one of the largest shopping centers in the United States.
- ❑ Supervised field and office staff.

FRANK NIVEO

Pueblo Properties   (1986–89)
Tucson, AZ
<u>Director of Leasing</u> (1988–89)
<u>Project Manager</u> (1986–88)

- ❏ Personally solicited over 50% of the company's clients within the last two years.
- ❏ Represented national tenant that required 10,000–12,000 square feet. Responsibilities included but were not limited to marketing strategies, site selection, and lease negotiations.
- ❏ Responsible for all feasibility reports, including analysis of consumer market, retail market, traffic patterns, proposed layouts and proposed tenant mixes. Reports were geared toward potential shopping center sites and older centers that required new leasing strategies.

Valley Center   (1984–86)
Prescott, AZ
<u>Project Manager</u>

- ❏ Responsible for leasing of all properties in medium-sized shopping center.
- ❏ Negotiated all contracts.
- ❏ Prepared marketing materials.
- ❏ Actively solicited tenants.

PERSONAL

- ❏ Fluent in Spanish, written and spoken (including all relevant legal terminology).
- ❏ Member, National Association of Real Estate Developers.
- ❏ Member, National Association of Shopping Center Planners.
- ❏ Volunteer coach, Mesa "Bobcats" youth soccer team.

Note: Frank knows what employers in his field look for when they review resumes. He has described his experience in terms that employers find appealing. Of course, this resume will have to be reformatted to be successfully "scanned."

STEVEN NYUGEN

Home: 18527 Forest Way
Mercer Island, WA 98040
206-493-1339

Office: Seattle Pacific Park
1442 Olympia Blvd.
Seattle, WA 98188
206-244-4466

SUMMARY

Financial Services Executive offering extensive background in Cash Management, Accounting, Portfolio Management, Client Services, and Money Market Management.

QUALIFICATIONS

- Extensive knowledge of money and capital market instruments, bonds and commodities.
- Direct sales experience with institutions.
- Proven record of success developing new business in highly competitive markets.
- Quality-driven professional who can reorganize functions and retrain personnel to achieve and exceed management goals.

SELECTED CAREER HISTORY

Manager: Money/Cash, Seattle Pacific Bank
Seattle, WA 1990–present

- Function at Vice-Presidential level in state's largest independent bank.
- Report directly to the Controller and President. Recruited as a troubleshooter to supervise a staff of nine professionals in order to correct many outstanding transactions.
- Established a new process to investigate, reconcile, and improve accounting entries. Recovered over $500,000 in lost revenue.
- Assured accurate banking reserve account status and efficiently controlled balances in banking reserve accounts.
- Controlled major cash flow. Upgraded control and administrative standards, enhancing bank profits through the use of improved procedures.
- Instituted new cross-training programs for bank personnel in complex clerical and administrative procedures.
- Monitored reports to senior bank management and regulatory authorities, assuring compliance, accuracy, quality and timeliness.

STEVEN NYUGEN
Page 2

Money Position Manager/Investment Portfolio Securities Manager
Tacoma National Bank, Tacoma, WA 1984–90

- Began as Investment Portfolio Securities Manager, preparing and processing corporate portfolios of federal, state and municipal bonds.
- Promoted to Money Position Manager, responsible for forecasting the company's lawful reserve requirements based upon $200 million of cash flow, relaying financial data to the Federal Funds Traders, and coordinating activity with internal and external bank executives.
- Maintained and controlled liquidity reserves and managed cash.
- Designed improved methods for obtaining instant cash position.
- Managed tax allocation program.
- Traded time deposits with foreign banks.
- Interfaced personally with key customers.

EDUCATION

M.B.A., Finance, University of Washington
B.A. Economics, Evergreen State College, Olympia, WA

PERSONAL

Very active in local community. Have served as officer of numerous organizations,including Mercer Island Little League, Mercer High School Parent-Teacher Organization, Volunteers in Service to Seattle, and Friends of Mercer Island Medical Center.

Note: Here is a person with a high-level job who is faced with the same challenges every resume writer faces: communicating clearly the skills and qualifications he brings to a new job.

Samuel Reuben
1938 N. Collins Ave.
Miami Beach, FL 33109
305-697-8810

PROFILE

Results-oriented, technically-trained, management-experienced professional seeks position where entrepreneurial abilities will be welcomed.

QUALIFICATIONS

- Talent for developing new business
- Capable liaison with both managers and technical staff
- Broad-based experience in private industry, government, and overseas businesses
- Certified professional engineer, with specialties in mechanical and electrical engineering
- Skilled project manager, with background in large-scale applications

ACCOMPLISHMENTS

Miami Urban Transport
- Project engineer for innovative light rail system

Newark Airport Monorail
- Project manager for state-of-the-art-automated transportation system

Baltimore Harbor Expansion
- Associate project manager for 3-yr. harbor dredging program

Korean Nuclear Agency
- Co-designed redundancy logic system for multi-million dollar nuclear power plant in Seoul, Korea

Texaco Refinery Expansion
- Consulting engineer for $3 million expansion of oil refinery in Kuwait City, Kuwait

EDUCATION

M.S., Electrical Engineering
   Pennsylvania State University
B.S., Mechanical Engineering
   University of Michigan

Note: Available to work as full-time employee or freelance consultant. Extensive portfolio and references available upon request.

Note: Sam demonstrates that dates are not essential on a resume! He has written an impressive resume without a single date!

200

Georgette W. Jackson
2124 Richland Drive, Apt. 3
Columbia, South Carolina 29201
(803) 698-4738

OBJECTIVE

Position in Computer Service where I can contribute my extensive training and experience in software, networking and hardware.

STRENGTHS

- Experienced in installation and maintenance of UNIX-based file servers and workstations.
- Skilled in installation and maintenance of all network components including routers, bridges and cabling.
- Trained in installation and maintenance of NOVELL fileservers, routers, printservers and networks.
- Expect NOVELL certification as a Network Engineer in June 1994.
- Hardware experience includes PC-based and FileNet proprietary fileservers and workstations, disk drives, tape drives, bridges, scanners, laser printers, robotic devices and Tandem mainframes.
- Troubleshooting and maintenance work with ORACLE and other databases.
- Software and hardware troubleshooting and problem resolution skills.

EXPERIENCE

Multisystems Corp. San Jose, CA
System Support Engineer
- Responsible for accounts in South Carolina.
- System level software and hardware support in a UNIX-distributed operating environment. (8/94–Present)

Compunet, Inc. Sunnyvale, CA
Field Engineer
- Responsible for client base in Southeastern states, trouble-shooting on Tandem mainframes, CDC disk drives, work stations, and printers.
- Began as Associate Field Engineer; promoted within six months to Field Engineer. (7/93–7/94)

EDUCATION

Honors Graduate, DeVry Technical School, 1993

Note: It is often difficult for computer programmers to develop easy-to-read resumes. Georgette pinpoints her skills by specifying the hardware and software she is capable of using.

Steven Noonan

1330 Pine Grove Ave., #210
Mobile, AL
(205) 793-8802

QUALIFICATIONS

- Skilled electrical engineering technologist with more than 5 years of progressively responsible, hands-on experience.
- Understands quality assurance procedures in electronics manufacturing.
- Uses computerized databases and tracking software.
- Works effectively as member of team or independently.
- Goal oriented. Comfortable with production quotas.

EXPERIENCE

Precision Electronics, Mobile, AL
Manufacturer of solid-state components for aircraft flight control. Subcontractor for major corporations, including Lockheed, McDonnel-Douglas, and Martin Marietta. (1990-present)

Engineering Data Processing Analyst
- Responsible for developing and modifying engineering databases for reporting and analyzing data within component and materials engineering departments.
- Prepared reports to support engineers and engineering management.
- Investigated component and material failures using all available computer and paper file systems as needed.
- Interfaced closely with Quality Assurance in disposition of Receiving Inspection rejections.

Electrical Technician/Planner
- Inspection Technician responsible for training new employees on computer systems, and in the practices andprocedures on the Receiving Inspection Department.
- Interfaced with Program Office, Purchasing and Engineering personnel to solve problems within the Receiving Inspection area.
- Developed and documented inspection plans using contractual, government and in-house requirements for all materials that passed through Receiving Inspection.

Steven Noonan
Page 2

EXPERIENCE

Electrical Inspector
- Performed electrical testing, data review, and visual inspection on all semiconductors.
- Maintained accurate part and vendor history files for government and in-house audits.
- Traveled to various vendor locations to perform pre-cap and data review inspections prior to shipment.

CERTIFICATES

- Inspection of Reliable Electrical Connections
- Inspection and Usage of Plastics
- Level I Radiographic Inspections
- ESD Certification

AWARDS

General Manager's Award
For developing and implementing a database for tracking materials and their manufacturers for purposes of traceability on government and commercial satellite programs.

EDUCATION

Electrical Engineering Technology
A.A.S., Bayport Community College
Prichard, AL
Recipient of "Outstanding Student in Technology" award, 1989

Note: This resume does a number of things well. It begins with a strong "Qualifications" section, articulates experience concisely, and includes both "Certificates" and "Awards."

Joanna Hope-Franklin
2139 Annandale Pkwy.
Falls Church, VA 22042
(703) 864-1793

PROFILE

Computer systems generalist with specialties in medical insurance and malpractice insurance.

ACCOMPLISHMENTS

- Worked with both internal and external customers to implement, develop and refine a medical malpractice policy rating, billing and collection system for 8,000 policies totaling $100 million in premiums
- Installed database system in 3 outside medical malpractice insurance companies providing ongoing service to external and internal customers
- Expanded the policy services system to include issuance and billing of corporate policies numbering more than 4,500
- Designed and oversaw development of system for tracking commissions payable to brokers, reducing expenses by more than 20%
- Worked closely with finance to ensure timely and accurate accounts receivable, resulting in reducing average collection time by 15 days

SKILLS

- Knowledge of Unix operating system
- Comprehension of DOS, Word Perfect 5.0, Lotus 1-2-3 on PC-based platform
- Knowledge of programming Languages: C and COBOL
- Strong oral and written communications skills
- Excellent administrative and supervisory skills

EMPLOYMENT

Supervisor, Department of Information, National Medical Underwriters, Alexandria, VA

Customer Service Liaison, National Medical Underwriters

EDUCATION

B.S., Biology, University of Virginia

Continuing Education courses in Management Information Systems, Department of Electrical Engineering and Computer Systems at George Washington University

Note: Here is a resume that does not have a section entitled "Experience," but the well-detailed "Accomplishments" and "Skills" will definitely get an employer's attention.

Joanna Hope-Franklin
2139 Annandale Pkwy.
Falls Church, VA 22042
(703) 864-1793

PROFILE Computer systems generalist with specialties in medical insurance and malpractice insurance.

ACCOMPLISHMENTS

Worked with both internal and external customers to implement, develop and refine a medical malpractice policy rating, billing and collection system for 8,000 policies totaling $100 million in premiums

Installed database system in 3 outside medical malpractice insurance companies providing ongoing service to external and internal customers

Expanded the policy services system to include issuance and billing of corporate policies numbering more than 4,500

Designed and oversaw development of system for tracking commissions payable to brokers, reducing expenses by more than 20%

Worked closely with finance to ensure timely and accurate accounts receivable, resulting in reducing average collection time by 15 days

SKILLS

Knowledge of Unix operating system

Comprehension of DOS, Word Perfect 5.0, Lotus 1-2-3 on PC-based platform

Knowledge of programming Languages: C and COBOL

Strong oral and written communications skills

Excellent administrative and supervisory skills

EMPLOYMENT

Supervisor, Department of Information, National Medical Underwriters, Alexandria, VA

Customer Service Liaison, National Medical Underwriters

EDUCATION

B.S., Biology, University of Virginia

Continuing Education courses in Management Information Systems, Department of Electrical Engineering and Computer Systems at George Washington University

Note: This is the "electronic" version of Joanna's resume. Note that it removes the bullets, highlighting, and italic type. This new version can be more easily "read" by a computer.

SAMPLE RESUME INDEX 20

Accountant: 127, 128, 148

Actor/Actress: 152

Administrative Assistant: 113, 124

Advertising Copywriter: 151

Air Conditioning Technician: 114

Aircraft Mechanic: 129

Alcohol Counselor: 144

Attorney: 119, 175

Auto Mechanic: 123, 206

Bank Teller/ Manager: 126, 130, 148

Biologist: 174

Bookkeeper: 148

Book Production Manager: 138

Buyer: 146

Carpenter, 131

Clerk-Stenographer: 124

Collection Administrator: 120

Commercial Artist: 158

Computer Consultant: 149, 154

Computer Programmer: 141, 149, 154, 201, 204

Computer Systems Supervisor: 176, 204

Construction Supervisor: 131, 173

Corrections Administrator: 188

Corrections Officer: 150

Credit Analyst: 120

Customer Service Specialist: 190

Dental Hygienist: 134

Drug Counselor: 144

Educational Administrator: 191

Electrical Engineering Technologist: 202

Electrician: 114

Emergency Medical Technician: 172

Engineer: 147, 169, 200

Executive Administrator: 180

Executive Manager: 182

Executive Secretary: 113, 124

Financial Officer: 164, 198

Firefighter: 172

Fitness Counselor: 142

Flight Officer: 136

Garage Supervisor: 168

Golf Professional: 192

Graphic Artist: 158

Industrial Engineer: 169

Insurance Claims Representative: 162

Lawyer: 119, 175

Legal Secretary: 135

Maintenance Supervisor: 121

Marketing Manager: 132, 159

Mechanic: 207

Medical Assistant: 145

Military Officer: 136

Nurse: 140

Paralegal: 135

Physician: 170

Physician Assistant: 160

Pipefitter/Plumber: 118

Plant Manager: 121

Police Officer: 122, 163

Professor: 153

Public Relations Writer: 111

Radio/TV Producer: 165

Radiologic Technologist: 186

Real Estate Developer: 196

Recreation/Resort Manager: 184

Restaurant Manager: 125

Sales Manager: 116, 132, 137, 179

Secretary: 113, 124

Security Officer: 133, 150, 163

Social Services Specialist: 161

Social Worker: 143, 194

Software Engineer: 141

Store Manager: 139

Teacher: 109, 153, 156, 191

Theater Manager: 166

Travel Consultant: 112

Veterinary Technician: 178

DO YOU NEED SOME HELP WITH YOUR RESUME?

Resumes That Get Jobs is specifically designed to help you write your own best resume, assembled in the way that is right for you. If you follow the suggestions and complete the worksheets, you should be able to design a resume that will go right to work for you.

It is possible, however, that you might have questions that you can't answer on your own. Some job seekers find that they need some expert advice or answers to personal questions. This kind of help is often available in your own community. If you're not sure where to start, take a look at your local telephone directory under the headings "Resume Preparation Services" and "Career and Vocational Counseling." Before you call, read through the questions below. They will help you make an informed decision about the kind of assistance that might be best for you.

QUESTIONS TO ASK OF RESUME PREPARATION SERVICES

1. Would you describe your services in detail for me?

2. Do the resumes you prepare include skills, qualifications, and accomplishments?

3. What is your usual process in preparing a resume?

4. What if I don't like the resume that you produce?

5. Do you have a variety of sample resumes that I can look over?

6. What are the fees for your services?

7. What additional charges might there be?

8. When can I schedule an appointment to meet?

9. How soon after that appointment can I expect to see a prepared resume?

10. Are you able to provide the names of clients I could call as references?

These questions are just suggestions. After using this book, most people will only need to have their resumes printed—and many will even print their own!